My Approach to
CHARACTER DANCE

Author's Note

It is pretty obvious that I am deeply in debt to a great many people in the profession. Repeatedly they gave me encouragement for continuing to work on and create my own system of character dancing. Dancers, choreographers, teachers, critics, directors of companies, schools and teacher's training courses from Hungary, Russia and Great Britain have helped me to believe that to stick to my ideas is worthwhile and I must persevere in working on my principles whatever the odds. All this aided me tremendously in the past and present.

In the narrative of this book, I have mentioned many of these people by name and their important roles concerning my work on this character system. Sadly, many of them are not with us any more, nevertheless I wish to express my gratitude to them as well as to all those who, fortunately, are still amongst us. I would also like to thank those many students and followers whom I couldn't mention personally in the text, but whose feedback, interest and diligent work helped me to develop the system to how it is taught in the Royal Ballet School today, and to write this book.

Maria Fay
London 2011

Maria Fay collection

Also by Maria Fay

Mind over Body:
The Development of the Dancer – The Role of the Teacher
Maria Fay's Floor Barre

Maria Fay's Floor Barre DVD

The Ballet Class VHS
Faults Corrections Perfections VHS

My Approach to CHARACTER DANCE

MARIA FAY

The Choir Press

Copyright © 2020 Maria Fay

All rights reserved. No part of this publication may be reproduced or transmitted in any form or by any means, electronic or mechanical including photocopying, recording or any information storage or retrieval system, without prior permission in writing from the publishers.

The right of Maria Fay to be identified as the author of this work has been asserted by her in accordance with the Copyright, Designs and Patents Act 1988

First published in the United Kingdom in 2020 by
The Choir Press

ISBN 978-1-911589-88-4

The image shown on the front page is Hungarian embroidery by Maria's mother.

The author and publisher have made every effort to trace the copyright holders of the images on pages 2 and 9 without success and welcome correspondence from copyright holders we have been unable to contact.

Front cover images:
Maria Fay
Photo: Charles Hedges/The Royal Ballet School Special Collections.

COPPELIA; Kristina Karaseva and Vitaly Biktimirov in the Czárdás
The Bolshoi Ballet at the Royal Opera House, London, July 2010
Photo: Nigel Norrington/ArenaPAL

Contents

Foreword by Amanda Maxwell   vii
Preface   ix

What is Character Dancing?   1
The History and Progression of Character Dance   5

PART I
The Evolution of My System   15

Stamp Your Feet   17
Where There's a Will   21
Fight if You Must   30
Slowly But Surely   35
Let Your Hair Down   42
Style Awareness   46
Who Cares What The Critics Say?   49
Dance Round The World   56
Which One is Which?   63
Inventiveness or Authenticity?   67
Dreams About Unity of Style   69
Fitting In   73
Character Dance Via Air Mail   80
Through the "Dark Ages" to the "Renaissance"   88

Part II
Description of Barre Exercises and Centre Practice Steps
for Character Dance Classes   97

Foreword
by Amanda Maxwell

The publication of this narrative marks the completion of the circle of Maria Fay's work in the U.K. since her arrival here as a refugee in 1956.

Having had a successful career as a dancer in Hungary she was, first and foremost, a classical teacher and coach of great importance working with many companies and schools world-wide.

Her experiences of helping so many dancers over the decades then led to the development of the Maria Fay floor barre, designed for purposes of daily strengthening, and when necessary, as a constituent of the rehabilitation process after injury. She has written extensively, and made films about these two strands of her work.

But, until now Maria had not addressed on paper the third, and very significant element of her contribution to our profession, which was the development of her particular way of teaching character dance to classical dancers. Today, just as decades ago when her mind first turned to this issue, artistically and technically this is an important strand of classical teaching. It took some time to persuade Maria that this work could be written about in a way that artists and their teachers would find valuable, as well as being important to have a record over and above that carried in the heads of those of us who advocate her methods. Disciples can interpret, cherish the principles and indeed bring new thinking, but at the end of the day we are not actually Maria herself.

Originally the master plan for this book was to publish both the narrative and an integral Benesh score, with Maria's annotations. Serious illness intervened, and in the interim caused by that it also became apparent that the complexities of such an ambitious project had dramatically multiplied. However the Benesh score exists (written by

Fiona Cater in 2009) and Anna Meadmore, archivist for the Royal Ballet School, and herself a former pupil of Maria's at the Royal Ballet School, has agreed that the Benesh score, plus a volume of the linked annotations can, in due course, become part of the resources made available for study in the reading room at White Lodge. In the fullness of time this resource may also be made available on-line through Maria's family.

As someone who had the good fortune to encounter Maria Fay as a thirteen year old, and benefited from her wisdom throughout my career, it is my privilege to have tried to help Sarah and Peter Kelen with this long overdue project.

Preface

I hadn't quite finished work on my book "Maria Fay's Floor Barre" when I started writing the script for a video version of it. Simultaneously, I had to organise everything needed for the filming. Although Dance Books Ltd had agreed to act as publisher and distributor for both book and video, it was still left for me to tackle the numerous difficulties connected with the video project.

I knew from earlier experiences that the making of a dance video is never going to run smoothly, but this time I had to be prepared for an extra load of problems. The financial funds needed to support my rather complicated plan turned out to be substantial. In this video I contemplated the use of a split-screen technique, so far not used in the dance video market. The idea was to do a whole system of movement regime and sample classes on a single videotape as well as to overcome, from the viewers' point of view, the disadvantages of a one-dimensional and somewhat claustrophobic media. This was one of the reasons that made me decide to shoot and edit the video in Greece where it was cheaper to produce.

All my thoughts and energy were totally immersed in the project and I could hardly think of anything else. One day, however, in connection with a completely different matter I telephoned Mary Clarke, the editor of *The Dancing Times*. After a short conversation she asked me how I was getting on with my new video. I tried to put my troubles and hilarious adventures in Greece in a nutshell. We were about to say goodbye to each other when she said: 'I know that at present you must be very occupied with your filming project, but I wonder whether you would consider writing another series of articles after you finish the video?'

'Nothing would please me more, but I'm afraid I just haven't got anything left to say!' I thought that I heard a faint chuckle on the other end of the phone as if she were saying, 'You? The infamous "chatterbox"; nothing to say? Unbelievable!' Of course, this was just my imagination; nevertheless, I felt I owed her some proper explanation.

'For several years you have given me a generous chance to say in *The Dancing Times* almost everything that I felt needed to be said as far as our art form is concerned which hasn't been stated in my previous two videos. Following these series of articles, I've had a further chance to elaborate and expand on these ideas in my two books and now in my third video. I've said it all! There isn't one decent idea left in my brain worthwhile to write about.'

'Oh, don't I just know this feeling! This is exactly how I felt after Clement Crisp and I finished writing our third book. However, I am sure that when you've finished your present project and had a little rest, you might think differently.'

Of course she was right. She must have known me better than I did myself. After the launch of the book and the new video I had some rest that I found useful but awfully boring. During this time, my ex-pupil, ex-ballerina, "ex-stimulator" and dear friend, Josephine Jukes, came for a short visit from Stockholm where she and her husband, Tim Almaas, were teaching. One of her first questions was: 'What is your next project?'

'That is exactly the question that everybody, including myself, keeps asking, but ...' I told her what I said to Mary Clarke. After hearing me out she became impatient, almost angry with me.

'What nonsense! I know you have lots of interesting problems to discuss. Just to mention one: how about teaching and choreographing character dance, one of your favourite "side–line" subjects? Or have you forgotten the time when you kept working on this matter passionately, teaching your own system for many years in the Royal Ballet School (still taught there by your followers) and all over the dance world. You were also choreographing for television, films, and ballet companies in Britain and abroad. Hundreds of dance teachers of several generations continue teaching your system, your choreographies. Shouldn't you share your experiences with new and future generations of dancers and teachers?'

'Well, I haven't thought about it in that way ... Also, it seems to me that the profession is losing interest in this subject.'

'I am sure that it is not quite so, but, if it is, perhaps raising their interest again might be highly necessary! I know from experience how I longed to study more and better character dancing and so did quite a few of us in English National Ballet. Remember? I always resented the fact that during the fifteen years you coached me in my classical technique and roles, we never had time to spend on character studies.' She suddenly looked at me with a teasing and challenging smile. 'On second thoughts, is it possible that lately you have abandoned these topics, being too occupied with all your other professional projects?'

'Maybe ...'

I started to sort out my thoughts and I realised that her challenging and scolding made sense. I recalled the remarkable interest in character dancing and character dance studies during the fifties, sixties and seventies. The numerous invitations I received to teach this subject matter in this country, Europe and elsewhere – from classical ballet companies, vocational (and non-vocational) schools, dance-teacher organisations, teacher-training courses, television and films – was the best proof of the profession's enthusiasm. Sadly, since I was busy with my engagements as a classical ballet-teacher and coach, I was able to satisfy only a small percentage of these invitations.

Character dancing in the correct style, in good taste and performed excitingly was always important in the old classical ballets as well as in some of the later epic works. Wherever I was invited as a guest ballet-teacher there seemed to be an interest in character dancing also. Nevertheless, it seems that in the last two or three decades this enthusiasm has decreased. The question arises: why?

I focused my thoughts and came to the conclusion that in order to find the right answer one should scrutinise a few important matters. Perhaps the time is right to "re-state" the importance of character dance and "re-evaluate" its position in the 21st century. Hopefully, an analysis of the situation of character dance in the past, present and the future might contribute to the work of new generations of dance society.

I mentioned this to some of my close friends in the profession, and they all found it interesting. Charles Hedges, the dance critic, who years ago was the first amongst my friends to animate me into writing, and has also helped constantly to "transfigure" my "Hungarian-English" into coherent English in all my previous efforts as a writer of articles and books, was the most encouraging. He generously offered to play the same role again and said: 'Character dancing is a fascinating subject. It must be one of the most colourful and endless studies for dancers, considering the vast number of nationalities and ethnic groups whose dance styles differ so widely from each other.'

'Indeed, but this is only the tip of the iceberg. There is much more to character dancing than just characterising differing nationalities in movements!'

This is why I decided to embark on "putting pen to paper" – or to use more contemporary wording, to place my word-processor in the interest of the dance community again.

What is Character Dancing?

∞⌇∞

During the last century, character dance studies were an important and popular subject matter in both vocational and amateur dance education. It was generally agreed that the curriculum of all vocational schools – whether their profile was classical, contemporary or musical theatre – should include character dance studies. Consequently, a few principal ideas developed in connection with this matter:

- Character dancing should be taught to students right from their early years of dance studies.
- The lessons should be spread out evenly throughout their entire schooling period.
- Expert teachers, who would willingly expand their knowledge by taking part at various suitable courses held in accordance, should teach the subject.

Most of the non-vocational schools – they teach at least 90% of junior and senior dance students all over the world – also found it important to include character dance studies in their timetables. Thousands of children and young adults all over the globe who love dancing, but for some reason or another are physically not suited for classical ballet studies, find great pleasure and fulfilment in learning character dancing. For example, the popularity of Spanish dance classes amongst amateurs of all ages is remarkable all over the world.

These open classes are usually held after working hours as evening classes, and when the day schools have finished, so people can easily attend them. Also, in various countries some of the ethnic minorities (Polish, Indian, Russian, Norwegian, Greek, Italian, Jamaican, Gypsy, Jewish, Mexican, Argentine and Cuban people settled in Europe or the USA) like to keep up aspects of their cultural identities. The first generation is keen to practise regularly their traditional folklore dances and also to teach them to the second and third generations of offspring in their community.

In Commonwealth countries, institutions of dance education (Royal Academy of Dancing, Cecchetti Society, Imperial Society of Teachers of Dancing, British Ballet Organisation), as well as many other similar organisations worldwide, recognised the growing interest in folkloric and character dancing. They commissioned professional experts to choreograph character dances to suit the differing age groups. These syllabi were integrated by the various institutions into their specific examination system and are taught at numerous congresses and refresher courses and conveyed, as well as examined, at various teacher training courses.

One would expect therefore, that if any dance teacher, trainee teacher, dancer, choreographer or critic were asked the simple question: 'What is character dance and why should vocational and amateur students study it?', one would get a simple and unequivocal answer. However, in reality this isn't quite so. I have been teaching the subject to many devotees and made it my business to ask this question at the beginning of our studies. Most of the time I found that, instead of getting a clear definition, we ended up in quite a muddle.

Though it seems that there shouldn't be much reason for this confusion, it is important that dancers and students understand what the purpose of their character dance studies is. After all they, as well as their character teachers, spend a lot of time and energy practising it during their entire student years and later as performers. One can't expect, however, for students and dancers to have a clear view on this matter if we teachers haven't got the right answers.

To achieve this perhaps we should ask ourselves a few questions – even if the answers may seem at first glance quite evident – and after defining the correct answers, the slightly foggy view might start to clear:

- Are folk dancing and character dancing just two different idioms for the same concept, or are they two entirely diverse ones?
- Does character dancing interpret only different nationalities, or

does it, within the national characterisation, also convey the emotions and typical behaviour of different human beings in various conditions?
- Why is it that some dancers and specific roles in professional life are categorised as "character dancer" or "character role" even though these have got nothing to do with any kind of national dancing (Rothbart in *Swan Lake*, the witch in *La Sylphide*, Coppélius in *Coppélia*)?

Folk dance is a cultural tradition that every nation, tribe and ethnic minority on the globe has from ancient times. It was through dancing that people found it easy and natural to capture the attention of the opposite gender; to celebrate special occasions of their life (weddings, coming-of-age to sexual maturity); to ask the gods at religious occasions for blessings, fertility, successful hunting, rain, fertile lands, and so on ... It was also a good way to "have a good time".

As social conditions became more sophisticated, people made their dancing richer and more colourful with various occupational dances (like herd-dance, shepherd-dance, cowboy-dance, hunter-dance, soldier-dance, etc.) All these types of folkloric dances, though in style completely different in each community, have in common that they came into existence as a natural result of people's everyday life. Depending on their past and present history, some communities still have rich and living traditions. Some however, due to the evolution of civilisation, lost a great part of them, or are left with just a handful of almost fossilised remnants.

In the first part of the 20th century, many ethnographers realised that the result of urbanisation and "modern life" was killing off folkloric traditions. They recorded what was still left from the music, singing and dancing traditions in the countryside amongst the older generation of peasants. Some composers, professional and amateur dancers were eager to help them in this valuable work. These collections were to become the basis of many creations in art forms like symphonic music, operas and operettas and, of course, in dancing.

Ballet masters inserted national dances into their ballet choreographies. These were choreographed for professionals with an aim to entertain and impress an "elite" public. Some of these creations were strongly based on folklore and others became more stylised according to the choreographer's taste, the story-line and the style of the accompanying music. These dances are not just plain copies of amateurs' self-entertaining national dances. They were created for, and danced by, professional artists on stage, and therefore they are "character dances".

It would be a logical conclusion to say that a "character dancer" is obviously a skilled professional dancer performing character dances. Alas, this is only half the truth. As the art form of classical, romantic and dramatic ballet progressed during the last two centuries, more and more roles were created within these ballets where the dancer had to portray and "characterise" all kinds of people. These roles demand a talent for acting, a theatrical personality often combined with high technical dance skill. Those dancers who excel in these qualities are also called in our profession "character dancer".

The History and Progression of Character Dance

In the early 19th century national character dance, as we know it today, was introduced into classical and romantic ballet productions with great success. Fanny Elssler, the great dramatic ballerina of the time, introduced the Spanish cachucha into Jean Coralli's *Le Diable Boîteux* and the Polish cracovienne into Joseph Mazilier's *La Gypsy*; Filippo Taglioni created the famous Scottish reel for the *corps de ballet* in his *La Sylphide*; August Bournonville in his ballet *Toreadoren* surprised his public with beautiful Spanish-style dancing, and in his *Napoli* he choreographed a most exciting tarantella. In his own version of *La Sylphide* he made an excellent example of how to "implant" Scottish national dancing into a romantic ballet.

During the following years it gradually became a tradition to build character dances into the structure of classical ballets and operas. In some ballets the character dances were performed in a "realistic" way – in national costumes, character boots and shoes and with traditional folklore in mind (as in Act 1 of *Coppélia*). During the second part of the 19th century there were many creations where character dances were performed in more stylised costumes and in ballet slippers for the male dancers and pointe shoes for the ladies. As a result these choreographies had to be danced in a strongly stylised and idealised manner (for example in *La Bayadère, Esmeralda, Raymonda,* and *La Fille du Pharaon*).

In Jules Perrot's *Esmeralda* the ballerina in the title role danced her famous solo with a tambourine and in an idealised Gypsy costume but *en pointe*. In this variation virtuosity dominates the style. In Saint-Léon's *Coppélia* one can find both: when in Act II Swanilda performs her Spanish and Scottish solos in Coppélius' workshop she uses just a few suggestive props to indicate the differing national character styles, and she dances them in her pointe shoes. However, these solos are choreographed with such skill that it is up to the performer's talent and feeling for style to leave the audience in no doubt about which nation's dances they are watching. In these cases national character dominates over technical matters. In contrast, in Act 1 of the same ballet the corps de ballet dances the Hungarian Csárdás and the Polish Mazurka in correct national costumes and boots, and together with the music, they strengthen the choreography's national character style.

In classical and romantic ballet creations, character dances became gradually quite popular with choreographers, composers and audience, and were used in a variety of stylisations.

From the 18th century onwards the usage of folkloristic elements was a phenomenon that enriched all art forms and especially music and literature. Composers from the 18th century to today created with artistic freedom, and used folklore as well as oriental elements to weave some bits and pieces from this inexhaustible reservoir into the fabric of the various musical forms. These elements were applied to their compositions very differently according to the creator's personality and individual taste, and to the fashionable ideas in the world of music at the times in which they were living. Some great composers used them in symphonic compositions[1]; others in virtuoso instrumental pieces;[2] many in songs and choruses.[3]

Certain composers placed a whole opera or ballet in a specific country and based the entire work on its folklore.[4] It was also a recognised and popular artistic practice to compose music that was based on a kind of "imagined" or "mock" national style. This made-up style became extremely popular from the time of Mozart, who composed masterpieces in a Turkish style, like his famous *Turkish March*, and, what's more, a whole opera, *The Abduction from the Seraglio*, most of which he invented himself. He was inspired by the jingling sound that

---

[1] Haydn, Mozart, Beethoven, Tchaikovsky, Smetana, Dvořák, Ravel, de Falla amongst them.
[2] Brahms, Liszt, Stravinsky, Bartók.
[3] Schubert, Schumann, Mussorgsky, Kodály, Britten and so on.
[4] Mussorgsky's *Boris Godunov* and *Khovanshchina*; Stravinsky's *Petrushka Firebird* and *Les Noces*; de Falla's *Three Cornered Hat*; Ravel's *Bolero*.

the popular Turkish military bands produced as they played different, metallic, percussive instruments. Classical music lovers became familiar with this so-called "Turkish" sound and didn't question its authenticity.

This artistic trend continued in the first part of the 20th century and there were several composers who created acclaimed operas, ballets, operettas and musicals with a similar approach.[5]

Literature, architecture, fashion-design, painting, sculpture and, of course, dance followed as the so-called "Oriental styles" were very much favoured. Choreographers of the same period embraced these ideas with pleasure. Using folkloric and oriental elements gave numerous possibilities to invent interesting, colourful and new movement images. Depending on the style of the music, the choreography of the character dances was created in the same style. When the music was based on a fairly authentic folkloristic national style, the dances were created accordingly (like the Csárdás and the Mazurka of *Coppélia*). When the music was composed in an imagined style (the Chinese, Spanish and Oriental dances of *The Nutcracker*) the dances were choreographed in the same manner.

Creating in the "mock style" gradually became a kind of tradition. For example, to portray Chinese people on the ballet stage, it was taken for granted that the dancers had to have their lower arms at a 90 degree angle vertical to their upper arms which were horizontal, while their hands were clenched in fists with first fingers pointing upwards. Although it is common knowledge that this movement image has nothing to do with either Chinese folklore or Chinese classical dance traditions, with the help of stylish costumes and programme notes everyone acknowledges and recognises it as "Chinese dancing"!

In the late 19th and the first part of the 20th centuries, ballet creations not only included several character dances, but also big parts of the narration, or even the whole story of the ballet, took place in some exotic

---

[5] The Rimsky-Korsakov/Fokine ballet *Shéhérezade*; the Polovtsian Dances in Borodin's opera *Prince Igor*; the 'Persian' style ballet in Mussorsgky's opera *Khovanshchina*; the 'Japanese' style in Gilbert & Sullivan's *The Mikado* and Puccini's *Madama Butterfly*; and 'Chinese' style in *Turandot*; the 'Egyptian' in Verdi's *Aida*; the 'Ceylonese' in Bizet's *The Pearl Fishers* and 'Indian' in Delibes' *Lakme* to mention just a few.

territory (*La Bayadère, La Fille du Pharaon*). Therefore in these choreographies the classical ballet technique is moulded with certain national characteristic images into a "mock character style" in the same way that the music, costumes and scenery are created.

Operas of the same centuries also included national character dancing. As the music composed for these dance inserts was often strongly stylised (*Prince Igor, Khovanschina, Aïda*), the choreographies had to be created in a similar manner. After all, who would have known the authentic dance traditions of the Tartars of the Middle Ages, the Persians of the 17th century or the Egyptians a few thousand years ago? The choreographers could rely only on drawings, reliefs, murals or engravings and then used their imagination. In some other operas (*Il Trovatore, La Traviata, Boris Godunov, Evgeni Onegin*) the music for the dance insert was based on national motifs that allowed the choreographers to create the dances in fitting style.

In the first years of the 20th century, with the launch of the Diaghilev Ballet, an unprecedented evolution started in the art of dance, which in turn affected the progress of character dance. The choreographies of Michel Fokine, Vaslav Nijinsky, Bronislava Nijinska, Léonide Massine and George Balanchine introduced an era that brought about a progress never seen before in the profession. Our art form changed beyond recognition. In some of their creations these choreographers turned away from long epic productions and fairy stories based on classical ballet technique, character dance and mime. The new ballets were built up in completely different ways from the traditional structure (*pas de deux, variations,* and *coda*). The compositions were much freer and so were the costumes. For example, in Nijinsky's *L'Après-midi d'un faune* the dancers portray Greek mythological figures, but the female dancers are never *en pointe* or in tutus and they don't use any movements from the classical ballet vocabulary. The choreographer has created completely new movement images for them, just as he did in *Le Sacre du printemps*, and his sister, Nijinska, achieved in her revolutionary work, *Les Noces*. In all these works the dancers are not in traditional classical ballet costumes and footwear, but in innovative designs.

Although in Fokine's *Les Sylphides* the principal male dancer represents a human being and all the other dancers are in his imagination as sylphs, this ballet must be considered a milestone in dance history in that it is without a story. It was also Fokine who started to choreograph one-act character-ballets like *Shéhérezade*, *Gayané* and *Dance Tartar* (from *Prince Igor*), *Petrushka* and *The Firebird*. In the art of dance a new genre was born. Massine continued this line with his *Le Tricorne*. These creations started character dancing's golden period. From this time its role wasn't only meant to be a colourful diversion within a full-length classical ballet production,[6] but it became entirely independent.

In America in the early years of the 20th century, jazz and tap dancing spread like wildfire. It started amongst numerous Afro-American amateur dancers and singers and later it was gradually raised to the highest professional standards by outstanding professional black entertainers, choreographers and teachers (great stars like Bill "Bojangles" Robinson, the Nicholas Brothers, Jeni LeGon among them). Even Nijinska was inspired to create her ballet "Jazz" to Stravinsky's "Ragtime" with syncopated rhythms and "Afro-American" costumes. Soon, when film, and especially "the talkies", became the popular new media, together with black artists some white American dancers became outstanding interpreters of this unique type of dance culture and created their own personal style (the Fred Astaire and Gene Kelly films spring to mind). These were influenced by the folkloric cultures of three different nations (African dancing, Lancashire clogging and Irish step dancing).

Apart from jazz and tap dancing another theatrical genre heavily influenced by an influx of new wave productions on both stage and film in the USA was the musical. It was in some of these (*Oklahoma*, *Seven Brides for Seven Brothers*, *Kiss Me Kate* and *West Side Story*) that quality character dancing was included. One of the pioneer choreographers for this type of dance production was the American dancer Agnes de Mille followed later by Jerome Robbins and Gene Kelly.

---

[6] *La Bayadère, Raymonda, La Fille du Pharaon, Coppélia, Don Quixote, The Nutcracker, Swan Lake*, etc.

With the appearance and evolving popularity of non-narrative and character ballets the scene was set for further reformation in Europe and America. New "dancer-choreographers" appeared on the dance scene coming from a variety of dance backgrounds. Their creations were therefore not only very different in style from all the previous classical ballet-choreographers' work, but also they differed strongly from each other's choreographic style.

Soon, in the 1920s, there were numerous new works born in which these dancer-choreographers used totally new movement-idioms and techniques that completely abandoned pointe shoes, corsets and balletic hair-dos. This new type of dance began in central Europe and was called *Bewegung Kunst* ("The Art of Movement" in German).[7]

This "free" style of dancing evolved with Isadora Duncan, who in her dancing and choreographies was inspired by ancient Greek paintings, murals and sculptures. She wore Greek tunics on stage, danced bare-foot and with her hair free-flowing. Her art influenced numerous choreographers in Europe, as well as painters and musicians all over the world.

Another young American dancer-choreographer, Martha Graham, was destined to revolutionise the art form. She built up a completely different technical approach from Duncan which she called "Contemporary Dance" and most of her choreographies conveyed dramatic stories. She has many followers who built their creativity on the basis of the "Graham technique" but developed it in their own personal style. The names of Merce Cunningham, Paul Taylor, José Limón and Robert Cohan are pre-eminent, and the list of the second and third generation of contemporary choreographers and dancers is endless.

Before and during the First World War, Duncan made quite an impression with her "free style dancing" in Russia. However, her influence was quickly nipped in the bud. In Russia the Bolshevik Revolution and its ideology declared the creations of these contemporary choreographers to be bourgeois decadence and, as such, harmful to the building of a socialist state. At the same time numerous amateur and

---

[7] Represented by artists like Rudolf Laban, Kurt Jooss, Mary Wigman, Jacques Dalcroze, Rosalia Chladek, Harald Kreutzberg, Hanna Berger and many other followers.

professional folkloric and character companies were encouraged and funded by the political regime. The decades leading up to the Second World War and after saw the flourishing of brilliant folklore and character dance companies, not only in the Soviet Union but also in all the so-called socialist nations behind the "Iron Curtain". Some of those professional companies, especially some from the Chinese, Korean and Soviet States, had extremely high technical and artistic standards.

There are many works of great artistic value that were created in the second part of the 20th century which used a mixture of classical and free movements to convey a narrative. These are the so-called "dramatic ballets".[8] Telling stories by using only contemporary vocabulary was also done by some contemporary choreographers – Graham, Kurt Jooss and Mats Ek. And continuing to the present day, in numerous dance-productions choreographers use a mixture of all types of movement elements and styles with entire freedom. In most of the works of Mark Morris, Pina Bausch, Matthew Bourne, Fred Astaire, Gene Kelly, MacMillan, Béjart, Roland Petit, Christopher Bruce, and Ek, whether with or without story telling, the techniques of classical ballet, contemporary dance, jazz, tap, ballroom dance and acrobatics are mixed. However, it is exceptionally rare for stylised character dance elements to be used.

In the West in the last couple of decades there has been an artistic trend, in the world of theatre and productions on film and television, of re-producing and modernising classic dramas and operas. Naturally, this tendency had a strong influence in the world of dance. As a result, many traditional ballets composed in previous centuries have been modernised, "re-choreographed", "re-dressed" and also "re-rooted" into later eras. There are more and more examples of presenting new productions of old story-ballets with the original music, but, instead of the classical ballet technique in which they were originally created, they are re-choreographed with a mixture of movement idioms according to the choreographer's personal choice.

---

[8] By Antony Tudor, Ninette de Valois, John Cranko, Frederick Ashton, Roland Petit, Janine Charrat, Jerome Robbins, Kenneth MacMillan, Maurice Béjart, John Neumeier, Birgit Cullberg, Mats Ek, just to mention the best known amongst them.

Often these "modernised" productions appear to express some different or more contemporary messages than the original.[9] In these versions the music of the original character dance compositions may be unchanged but the choreography is modernised and strongly stylised: in some more recent productions of *Nutcracker*, for example, used as a parody.

It is a matter for individual taste to decide whether the general "updating" of these productions was for better or worse. Nevertheless, from the character dance point of view, one might find that style-wise, hardly any of the new versions represent progress.

Perhaps the largest group of late 20th and 21st century choreographies are the ones where the choreographers use either classical ballet technique and movement images or a contemporary vocabulary – or mix the two with their individually created own movement-idioms – without telling any story. They let the public enjoy the movement images, their combinations, variations, dynamics and rhythms for their own sake.[10] These are often termed "abstract ballets".

In connection with the art form of dancing, when one hears the expression "abstract" used, one can not help wondering whether there isn't a need to find a more fitting and precise name for these type of works. There are art forms where the communication between the artist and the public is done through using static and inanimate materials. The painter uses paint and canvas; the sculptor and architect may use stone, wood, metal or clay; the composer has musical instruments. In all these cases the products of the artists also might be "abstract". However, the question arises: can any type of dance creation be called abstract at all?

Communication between the choreographer – the creating artist – and the public in our art form is only possible through the dancer's body. Can one imagine a more living and organic substance than the human body? Add to this the fact that all the movements of which the

---

[9] Bourne's *Swan Lake, Nutcracker, Cinderella*; Neumeier's *A Cinderella Story*, Morris's *Nutcracker*, Ek's *Giselle, Sleeping Beauty*; Deane's *Swan Lake and Nutcracker*.

[10] Balanchine, Frederick Ashton, David Bintley, John Neumeier, Jirí Kylián, William Forsythe, Hans van Manen, Merce Cunningham, Paul Taylor, Mark Morris, José Limón, etc.

human body is capable depend entirely on physiological, and therefore, material functions. Perhaps, instead of calling story-less dance creations "abstract" – whether they are done with classical, contemporary or mixed style technique – the French expression *l'art pour l'art* (art for art's sake) might be the accurate definition. These types of creations, by their nature, have no use for any character elements.

The choreographers of the latter part of the 20th century[11] changed the world of dance even more then their forerunners. Most of them did not insert in their creations character dances as such, but skilfully moulded them into their composition in a strongly stylised form.

For example, in MacMillan's *Mayerling* the crown prince's Hungarian friends dance throughout the entire ballet in a masterfully adapted national style, and in his *Romeo and Juliet* he made the Gypsy girls dance in a style that generally is recognised as Gypsy. In Bruce's *Cruel Garden* the strong Spanish flavour is unmistakable and in his *Ghost Dances* some South American folkloric elements are quite dominant. Ashton, in his masterpiece *La Fille mal gardée*, moulded into the story a clog dance, the male *corps de ballet*'s dance with sticks and the peasants' dance with sickles, and in his *Two Pigeons* the Gypsy girl's dancing – although *en pointe* – is unmistakably in the right style. Petit also moulded a Spanish style into his ballet *Carmen* (which is actually French through and through by author and composer).

In Soviet Russia choreographers continued creating full-length epic ballets.[12] To please the political regime and fit the ballets into communist ideology they had to build up their three-act works and use the movement imagery in the manner of old traditional, classical ballet creations, mimicking the old masters of previous centuries. Evidently, the character dancing within these creations still had to play a substantial role and their leading character dancers performed and acted their roles at the highest artistic level. Their status in the hierarchic ballet companies equals the "stars" of their classical ballet colleagues. At the same

---

[11] Cunningham, Cohan, Taylor, Morris, Kylián, Ek, Forsythe, Alvin Ailey, Tudor, Ashton, MacMillan, Cranko, Bruce, Béjart, Petit, Neumeier, Robbins, van Manen.

[12] *Stone Flower, Red Poppy, Romeo and Juliet, Fountain of Bakhchisarai, Flames of Paris,* etc.

time fabulous character dance companies flourished under the leadership of outstanding choreographers such as Igor Moiseyev.

It is obvious that since the time of Fanny Elssler character dance has progressed, changed, branched out and become sophisticated beyond recognition. Old traditions were broken and if any new rules have been made they were up to each choreographer's individual taste and knowledge in the field of character dance.

The defining boundaries between a character dancer and a classical or contemporary one are becoming less clear, and in many creations of our times they are completely indistinct. In turn this situation means that, even more than in the past, all professional dancers nowadays have to be prepared in their student years to be able to deal with these quite sophisticated tasks.

However, this cannot mean that during the few years of their studies they should be taught more existing national styles. Just the opposite! Perhaps, what we teachers should concentrate on is that they should study just a few differing national styles, but thoroughly. In other words, the clichés of "less is more" and "quality not quantity" are absolutely valid and necessary for teaching character dance for vocational students.

Studies have to be geared not only to raise the young dancers' technical standards but also to increase their ability to differentiate between style nuances. Therefore classes have to be well constructed, regular and systematic, not only in order to prepare their muscles and avoid injuries, but also to gain simultaneously an understanding of style differences.

Experience has proven that after learning a few styles in this thorough manner they will learn and gradually adapt other styles faster and better. They will become more observant and sensitive to all types of style differences, and it will help them not only in picking up easily the different national styles, but also to grasp all the differing personal styles of choreographers who use movement images freely from the many existing dance-techniques. In the average repertoire of all dance companies nowadays, performers are required to dance these multifaceted creations, so they should be prepared for these tasks in their student years.

Part 1
The Evolution of My System

Stamp Your Feet

∞⋄∞

As a young dance student I liked watching good character dancing. However, as an older pupil, I must confess with guilt and shame, I disliked doing character classes and so did my classmates. There were several reasons why the subject was so unpopular with us.

During each practice, our muscles became stiff, heavy and knotty, often even painful. This happened not only during and after the first few lessons – which would have been understandable when learning unusual movements for the first time – but it became a regular occurrence throughout our character dance studies. Some of us, especially the male students, complained also about painful knee and ankle joints. It was even more worrying that some students were actually injured during a character class.

Having these symptoms regularly, we were afraid that gradually the lessons would make us vulnerable to minor injuries that, alas, might develop into chronic ones. Understandably, as an injury is always every dancer's nightmare, our suspicions and dislike grew towards a subject that might cause it.

Those of us who managed to avoid serious injury or who believed in the popular but mistaken cliché: "dancers must learn to work through pain no matter what" kept on practising in these classes with the determination and energy expected from every "ideal student". However this exemplary way of working, even if one didn't get injured, brought to the fore other worries. We thought that if during the many years of student studies each character class creates such aching and stiff muscles, sooner or later one might end up with what one dreads most – over-developed, bunched up and ugly muscles.

The occurrence of this problem seemed to us logical. Every dancer desperately strives, from their earliest years of training and during their entire dancing life, to develop a slim-looking, supple, yet strong body with well-shaped and refined muscles. This is the first criterion for a dancer to get a job and especially a distinguished one. Perhaps it is understandable that the sheer probability of developing an unpleasant-looking body was even more frightening for a dance student than the possibility of injuries!

There was another important issue that caused further frustration in those of us who were not injured, and tried to work diligently and consistently in our classes. We learnt lots of steps as well as numerous set *enchaînements* that were great fun to do. However, we were not satisfied with just practising movements, or emulating our teachers' demonstrations without understanding the subtleties that actually created the differences between various national character styles.

We were sure that there must be more to good characterisation than just wearing character shoes, skirts and boots, clicking your heels, stamping the soles of your feet hard and loud, clapping your hands and "looking jolly". We felt that something quite important must have been missing from our interpretation without being able to put it into words. This led us to feel not only artistically unfulfilled but also rather muddled. If I had known then what I know now, I would have probably recognised what caused this problem: our bodies were moved but our minds and spirits were left untouched.

As if these problems weren't enough to turn us against character dance studies, we developed an additional aversion, as graduation grew closer. Some of our friends, who had already graduated from school into professional companies, condescendingly informed us: 'It is a great mistake when a graduating student performs outstandingly in the character classes. You get pigeonholed as a character dancer for the rest of your professional life!'

It didn't even occur to us that this statement might have been based on quite dodgy evidence and perhaps it could be the result of some kind of "sour grapes". We believed it to be true, and panicked.

Students get used to the fact that if someone's body isn't a hundred percent turned out or well proportioned, supple and slim or is too small or too tall, they can hope only to be a character dancer. So, to become one – even if one achieved soloist rank – was in our eyes just second best, lowering our ambitious dreams. Every classically trained student hopes to excel first of all as a classical dancer. Also, which young dancer would want to be pigeonholed at that stage of their young life? Being categorised, even before being given the chance to try one's wings on a wider scale and find one's real talent and stage personality, seemed unfair.

Although we were fond of our character teachers and didn't want to hurt their feelings, none of us wished to run the risk of getting injured or, even worse, to have ugly and unsuitable muscles and – on top of it all – to be constrained into a pigeonhole.

NO, NO, NO! We thought, this mustn't ever happen to US!

We were convinced that we must do something in order to avoid this situation. So, with the "infinite wisdom of teenagers", and by listening to the advice of some of the cynical or bitter elements, we tried to find ways to sabotage lessons without it being too obvious. We used to alternate "tactics" in order to cover up this fact. We found acceptable excuses to skip class (like claiming light injuries, a dentist appointment, migraine, food poisoning, period pain, name it!) When taking part in the class, we avoided working full out and did the exercises in a more or less "wishy-washy", undedicated manner.

We didn't know that all these "sabotage tactics" were quite well known "students' tricks" and our teachers could see through them. Nor did we fully understand how wrong our attitude was and that what we did was first and foremost our own loss. It occurred to a few of us how much we must have hurt, disappointed and frustrated our hardworking character teachers, but we convinced ourselves that our actions were justified. Ignorance and immaturity can be amazingly cruel!

It was some years later when it started to dawn on me that the roots of all our problems – physical and artistic – might have been hidden in the construction of these character classes. Perhaps the emphasis should have been put on not how much and what was taught to us, but rather on how the classes were built up technically and style-wise.

When I finally gave up dancing and had the chance to teach all over the dance-world, I realised that these situations existed not exclusively in my own school and country, but were quite typical in many vocational schools elsewhere.

It became obvious to me that this state of affairs was wrong and harmful in the progress of our art form. I felt that perhaps there might be something one could do in order to find a solution to this unfortunate situation and change it for the better.

Where There's a Will …

My curiosity about character dancing was aroused when, as a young dancer, I saw for the first time on film the Kirov Ballet dancing *Swan Lake* and the Bolshoi Ballet in *Don Quixote*.

The delightful elegance, ease and expressiveness with which the exquisitely trained dancers performed the character dances within these ballets impressed and surprised me more than anything else. They expressed not only the diverse nationalities but, with refined characterisation, they gave the audience all sorts of dramatically important information: court etiquette, social status and human relationships which helped to illustrate the story within the ballet.

A little later some specialised dance companies from the Soviet Union visited Hungary: the Moiseyev, the Pyiatnizky, the Georgian and the Red Army. I saw a few of their magical performances and I realised that they were not just pleasing theatrical exhibitions about the different folk dances of the Soviet Union's several ethnic communities, they became further eye-openers.

The dancers' technical virtuosity, combined with refined artistic quality and musicality, expressed various human emotions, situations, occupations and different relationships. The characterisations of young or old figures were comical, serious, tragic, heroic, determined, angry, happy, lazy, and diligent. They were all there as colourful as the paints on an artist's palette. I was eager to see more, especially from the work of the Moiseyev Company. However, they performed when I was performing myself, so I asked permission to observe some of their daily classes and rehearsals, which they generously granted. Having a chance to get an insight into their daily routine was a further revelation.

The dancers were highly disciplined, their exciting technical skill was due to a specific exercise regime of well-structured classes based on classical ballet practice, but with great emphasis on the Russian national style. This was taught in the company's vocational school. With the exception of a few of the older artists they had a slim, pliable and pleasing muscle structure. I enjoyed watching their rehearsals and felt an urge to get up from my chair to join in, to become part of them. From this time on, whenever and wherever I had a possibility, I studied the work of these and other companies with a similar profile.

Seeing my eagerness, some ensembles – especially the Moiseyev and the Georgian – invited me at times to join in their daily classes. I just fell in love with what I saw and learned from them and this "love affair" has lasted during the rest of my life. (This was a far cry from the student days when I disliked, and "sabotaged", my character and folklore studies!) Little did I know that, years later, my interest in this kind of dancing was going to play an important role in my professional life.

After the Second World War – in Hungary as well as in the other "Iron Curtain" countries – there were numerous professional, semi-professional and amateur folklore dance companies. Even in the professional ensembles, most dancers and choreographers didn't have any previous vocational schooling. With some exceptions their performances struck me as somewhat amateurish. There was no comparison between the artistic and technical level of the Soviet character-dance companies and that of ensembles belonging to the Soviet satellite countries. I came to the conclusion that this great difference must be rooted mainly in the dancers' structured schooling.

A few years later, I was critically ill with meningitis and encephalitis. For the first two months the doctors had serious doubts whether I would ever be able to dance again, but I was adamant to prove them wrong. My recovery was slow. I was confined to bed for months. Lying there day and night with closed eyes (daylight and artificial light were equally unbearable), I became inpatient with wasting so much time. I wanted to find some kind of occupation connected with dancing that could be achieved in this situation (what a desperate task!) which would take my thoughts away from my miserably bleak-looking present.

It was in the seventh week of my illness that one night – instead of the usual feverish nightmares – I had a pleasant dream. It included several fragments of various epic classical ballets including some of their character dances. As often happens in dreams, this vision got muddled up with broken images from the Moiseyev Company's repertoire. After I awoke and my mind gradually cleared, an idea started to develop. The imagery of the Moiseyev character dancing so impressed me that I thought perhaps one could create a structured practice regime for the Hungarian style as well as the ethnic minority groups that lived in Hungary. This should enhance young dancers' character dance technique without causing physical injuries, as well as improve the artistic interpretation of Hungarian folklore and character dances. I kindled this idea for a while and later I told my husband about it. When I said that I wanted to start working on it right there and then in the hospital he looked alarmed. He must have thought that it was some feverish delirium that made me irrational, and anxiously told my doctor about it.

'We must wait and see,' the doctor said, 'but hopefully, her determination to make her brain function is not an indication of a deteriorating mind, rather a positive sign of progress.'

'But how?' my husband wondered and – quite frankly – so did I. To quieten his agitation (and my own) I said to them: 'Well, where there's a will, there's a way. I just have to find it.'

'That kind of positive outlook might be a great help in your recovery', remarked the doctor and left me to it. It was easy for me to quote such a wise proverb but less straightforward to make it work!

I was aware that before I could start on the practical part of the project (exercises at the barre, in the centre and so on...) there was a lot of theoretical work to do. I first had to work out the correct structure on which I should build my system, but even before this, I had to define what the real Hungarian style was. Fortunately, this preparation was theoretical work and didn't require any physical involvement. The dilemma was much more complex than one would have thought. At the time there was quite a muddle concerning this.

In Hungary's music and dance culture there exist several entirely different styles – the Hungarian palotás (Hungarian Court dance), Hungarian folkloric and quite a collection of similar traditions that belonged to different minor ethnic groups living in the country: Gypsy, Croatian, Serbian, Romanian and Slovakian.

Palotás were dance-forms and movement images which were suitable for the nobility to dance in the palota (palace). These stylised, elegant movements that had been "made to measure" by dancing masters in the 18th and 19th centuries suited the court manners as well as the elaborate costumes and head-dresses. Although these movements had some Hungarian flavour, they had very little to do with Hungarian folklore. However, ballet choreographers all over Europe found this artificial style a suitable foundation on which to base their theatrical versions, such as in *Coppélia, Swan Lake, Raymonda,* etc. Non-Hungarian speaking choreographers, as well as composers, named all Hungarian dances "czárdás". In the Hungarian language the word "czárda" means pub. So the dance form, as well as the steps which were danced in pubs and taverns, became known as czárdás. Nobody belonging to the nobility would have set foot in such places, let alone danced in them!

The spelling of the words "czárda" and "czárdás" was changed two centuries ago to "csárda" and "csárdás". In these places only people of the lower classes – peasants, serfs and some young bohemians – gathered to have a good time: drinking, folk-dancing, singing and playing folk music. This was the real Hungarian csárdás, matching the folkloric beauty and simplicity of other functional Hungarian traditional (eg wedding) and occupational dances (shepherds, swineherds, cowboys, cooks, soldiers, etc.). Style-wise this was completely different from the elegant and theatrical "palotás" or court dances.

The Gypsy tradition was another fascinating dance and music culture in Hungary. This had hardly anything in common with Hungarian folklore. The Gypsies had their own specific music and movement images that were extremely colourful and dramatic, with many mood and speed changes. Their traditional life style, often "mystified" by romantic writers, was also very different from that of their adopted country (wherever that might be), and suitable for the professional stage. As most of the Gypsies made their living by playing music in pubs, restaurants and hotels, with fabulous virtuosity they often mixed the music of Hungarian minority groups (Romanian, Slovak, Serbian) with traditional folk music of their own. This mixed style is often mistaken for Hungarian folkloric music. The dance and music culture of other, various ethnic minorities with their exciting rhythms, floor-patterns and costumes also provide a strong contrast to Hungarian folklore and Hungarian Court styles.

I was convinced that in the artistic maturation of young vocational students it would be crucially important to study all these differing dance styles, providing that they could be conveyed in a well-structured way that would avoid injuries. To achieve this goal I started to work out a system based on these principal ideas for a simple style and technique of Hungarian folk dance tradition. Once that was achieved the other styles would follow.

Having cleared all the existing muddled ideas about the Hungarian style I could start to work out the structure of my system. As a model I chose the build-up of a classical ballet class. In my eyes this traditional system was the best and most precisely constructed exercise-system; for centuries it has produced the majority of professional dancers. Another reason for this choice was a practical and logical one, to make character dance studies more approachable for ballet-trained students.

The next step in this theoretical work was to establish some principle ideas:

- Each lesson must start with a barre exercise similarly built up as in a ballet class.
- The barre exercise – contrary to the customarily taught "multiple-styled" character barre – should be done in the same style as the rest of the class. Rather like when learning a foreign language for the first time; within one class one is studying only one language, concentrating on its correct pronunciation, spelling, grammar and even the logic of its grammar. One doesn't learn several languages within the same lesson. "Warming up" the muscles of the body with the barre exercise has a vitally important physical purpose in the dancer's life in every kind of movement regime, whether it is in studying classical ballet, contemporary studies, tap or jazz dancing. If, simultaneously, it is used as a tool through which the given style, its typical punctuation of movements and its relationship to the music can be enhanced, it makes not only common-sense to do so, but it will lead to the required quality.

- The accompanying music must match the style of the class.
- One national style should be studied completely for at least one term (if necessary even two) before learning another.
- To enhance co-ordination and the correct style, the head, arm and torso movements must be added to the barre work right from the beginning of studies.
- In the centre practice the students should first learn the various steps they have prepared for at the barre. (As with a foreign language: first one learns a few simple words, with correct pronunciation and accent. For dancers a step equals a word, the way it is danced equals the pronunciation.)
- The steps should be put into simple *enchaînements*. (After learning some words, one makes simple sentences with them).
- The combination of steps should be danced in specific floor patterns that are typical of the required style (circles, lines, couples holding on to each other by the hands, shoulders, waists, and so on). At a later stage these *enchaînements* or "études" should become longer and more complicated. (Staying with my simile: like creating a paragraph and later an essay).
- Professional students should learn some dances from the repertoire or specifically choreographed compositions suitable for stage performance, while amateur students should learn some traditional folk dances. (Like learning a poem or reciting a part in a play).

For vocational students, dancing in the Hungarian folkloric style is not physically demanding. Therefore, I thought that this was perfect for junior pupils. It seemed to offer an opportunity to teach them to dance without the sophistication of classical ballet and historical dancing, and to express various human qualities, moods, sentiments and relationships with simplicity and freedom. As folk dancing is mostly executed in larger groups and with explicit floor-patterns, the youngsters would benefit from learning how to dance by relating their movements to each other and keeping precise distances while moving in given patterns. (A good preparation for *corps de ballet* work.) I realised also that these basic principles – studying one national style in one block, and my sketch for a class of a balletic structure – could become a general model for character dance teaching of any nationality.

With my theoretical preparation I achieved a fairly enabling framework, and the next task should have been to fill out this frame with details first in the Hungarian peasant style, following it up with other national styles. However, I had to be patient as I was still bed-ridden and my progress of getting healthy seemed to be terribly slow. When I was allowed to sit in a chair twice a day for five minutes only, I used these sessions to make some notes on my theory. Then, in the following week, supported by a nurse, I was allowed to do a few steps. I must have looked more like a dizzy drunkard than a dancer, not exactly the ideal condition to create physical exercises, but I was not to be beaten by "temporary difficulties". I didn't forget my motto: "Where there's a will, there is a way ..."

Lying in bed I hummed some folk tunes. I imagined several movements and tried to execute them with my fingers or my arms. When I found a satisfactory exercise I memorised it. Then, I created the next one and memorised that and when I had my "sitting session" I made some further notes. The nurse would take me in a wheelchair daily to the bathroom, where the huge old-fashioned hospital bathtub was large enough for me to do some of the imagined exercises in a horizontal or sitting position. Afterwards, lying in bed I continued doing them as long as the covering blanket didn't give my "sins" away. I discovered a few interesting facts.

This was the first time that I realised how much strength and pliability a dancer can regain by exercising in a lying or sitting position and in water. (I made use of this discovery later in my career when I helped injured dancers during their rehabilitation period and eventually created my Floor Barre system.) Also, who would have thought that a bathtub filled with water, a hospital washbasin or a bedstead could become a "perfect" ballet-barre? Only a dancer with a "slightly damaged brain". I almost enjoyed the fact that a critical illness of the brain should offer the right atmosphere for creating the theoretical and practical background of a new dance system!

A few months later – still during my recuperation period – I told an ex-colleague and friend of mine who had an influential position in the

Ministry of Culture, all about my system. She rather liked the whole concept I was working on. I was granted a small sum of money to hire a professional typist and make a record of my work, which existed up to that point only partly in my scribbles and partly in my movement memory.

It would be quite a few more months before I was able to dance on stage again, so I petitioned for, and gained, a short sabbatical leave. During that time I started to do daily classes and took up swimming in order to get more strength and stamina. Also, I was dictating to a typist the theory of my character system as well as the detailed exercises. After gaining permission from the Hungarian State Folk Dance Company, I watched and studied regularly their daily work, rehearsals and performances. This was an invaluable help to complete my "vocabulary" and to polish the style of the Hungarian peasant and Gypsy dances. This was complemented further by studying also with other experts on Hungarian, Romanian, Croatian and Serbian folklore.

By the time I was able to return to the stage and start performing, I had finished, more or less, the basic work of the first part of my character system: the Hungarian peasant style. Still, I was painfully aware that the most important factor – the "proof of the pudding" – was still missing. My work had to be taught to young ballet students in order to see how it worked in practice.

One of the ballet-mistresses in the State Theatre, who was also the directress of a vocational ballet school, came to my rescue. She asked me to teach my character system twice a week to the 14/15 year-old students. They liked the classes and were keen to do them, whilst I had the benefit of realising where changes were needed.

After a few months the Ministry of Culture insisted that these students should give a demonstration to a few experts in charge of character teaching in vocational schools. (In the communist regime one couldn't teach any system without official approval.) One of these experts was an ex-ballerina, Karola Szalay. They – especially Miss Szalay – seemed to be delighted with what they saw and so they gave me the "go ahead"... and so I did. I wanted to find out how the 10/11 year-olds would react to this subject. I just simplified and shortened the *enchaînements* both at the barre as well as at centre practice. I was amazed when I saw the result after a few weeks of studying. Not only did the children pick up the movements exceptionally well, but, from the style point of view, these youngsters were better and faster than their seniors. They just danced with a natural, uninhibited simplicity and charm.

I was still determined to extend my system to the various other styles but I became much too busy to do this work properly. Apart from dancing with my company, I had been invited to guest-perform as well as to choreograph in another theatre. Before premieres I had to stop teaching, so detailed work on various ethnic styles had to wait for quite a while.

Fight if You Must

∞⌒∞

During the period I spent on polishing my character system and teaching it to the younger pupils, the Moiseyev Company visited Hungary again. This time I was determined not only to study their wonderful work but to consult Moiseyev himself, if he agreed, and show him what I'd done so far. I have admired his work more than anybody else's in the field of character dancing, and I felt that his opinion and criticism would be the best guide in furthering the work concerning my character dance system.

I was a bit worried though, for how would I manage to get an appointment for such a discussion? I wanted to avoid going through the security check so typical of the Soviet and Hungarian communist bureaucracy at that phase of the Cold War. The procedure – even if I was granted permission – could have taken longer than the Moiseyevs' stay in Budapest. I had to be cunning.

This time the company was staying for a few weeks in Budapest and their living quarters were in a hotel on St.Margaret's island, situated in the middle of the Danube not too far from the theatre where they performed. I decided to go there and try to find Moiseyev and his interpreter ... but what would be the right time for doing so? I knew that after first-night celebrations, touring dance companies – management included – would never start the next day's work at an early hour. So, the following morning I went quite early to the hotel, making sure that everybody from the ensemble was still there. On arrival I sat down in the hall and read a book for about an hour. Then I went to the reception desk and boldly asked the hotel porter to contact the company's interpreter. Luckily, she knew who I was and promised to try to arrange an appointment for me with "the Boss" during the following days. When we finished our conversation and I was about to leave, Moiseyev himself appeared looking for her. Seeing us together he seemed to remember me (what a memory!), and after listening to my plea he said in a charming manner: 'I will be much too busy during the following weeks. I have now about 20 minutes, so we might as well just do it here and now.' He ordered some black coffee, indicated to the interpreter and myself to sit by a table with him, and encouraged me to start.

I tried my best to explain my ideas in words but I felt rather frustrated, as the conversation through the interpreter seemed to me very awkward and slow. Secretly I glanced at my watch and realised that, if we were advancing so clumsily, there might not be enough time for me to tell – and show – him even an eighth of what I wanted to, let alone for him to give me his opinion and advice. So, without thinking what I was doing, I jumped up from the armchair and continued talking and demonstrating the movements at a speed the poor interpreter could hardly keep up with:

'For example, this authentic step from this and this dance looks like that', and I demonstrated a so-called "tükör-csárdás"(mirror-csárdás). 'So, I prepare it at the barre in the *battements tendus jetés* this way' (using the backrest of my abandoned chair as a barre and humming a suitable folk tune, my demonstration followed). 'Later I might add a *port de bras* and perhaps a wave of a handkerchief' (picking up a napkin from the table). 'Then, I'd teach it in the centre within a simple e*nchaînement* like this' (changing to another tune, my demonstration continued). 'Afterwards, I'd teach this basic movement with some simple variations like a "theme and variation".' (I was talking, dancing and singing.) 'Following these variations I'd create a continuous turn in the diagonal.' He nodded and smiled understandingly. Though the hotel lobby's highly polished parquet floor, furnished with Persian rugs, heavy armchairs and tables, wasn't exactly the most professional studio to show diagonal turns, there was nothing to stop me from showing them to him!

Quickly I rolled up two carpets and at the same time I carried on talking, then singing and turning in the rather small diagonal space I'd cleared. No wonder his smile changed into a good-humoured chuckle when I continued the "show" like a lunatic: 'One can combine this turning version for the girls with single *tour en l'air* and perhaps with *doubles* for the boys. I could also embroider this version for the girls by adding some claps like this: "la-la-lalala", and for the boys clapping on their boots after they land from the *double tour*: "lalalalala la-la".' I finally finished my obsessed demonstration. Suddenly I heard applause that came probably from some amazed hotel guests. I believe by now everybody in the lobby, including the porters, waitresses, etc., had had a good laugh.

Moiseyev smiled and nodded while he said 'Very good. It seems to me that you are on the right track. Can you show me a bit more?' I was in seventh heaven! I thought that after this "vivacious" introduction it was better to choose one of the most often-used steps in Hungarian folklore called "rida" that had many versions and was often performed at a slow tempo with a lyrical characterisation, but also had many fast and dynamic forms. I danced for him the basic step by itself. Afterwards I put it through the same progression as I did with the previous one. I also indicated how this step could and should be practised when dancing in couples as well as in circles or in lines.

I was sure that by then the 20 minutes he promised me must have been gone a long time ago, but he kept nodding and smiling and saying 'yes' or 'very good' or 'fine' (I didn't need the interpreter for these words). My heart leapt and nearly jumped out of my chest with happiness.

I mentioned to him that I wished to extend my work to the Hungarian Court style as well as working on the various ethnic styles to be found in Hungary. He became especially interested when I mentioned and showed him just a few typical movements from the Gypsy dances existing in my country, and how I wanted to teach this tradition within the structure of my system. I also explained to him that basically I designed my whole system as well as the build-up of every class, in the way that classical ballet studies are structured. Although I wished to keep the purity and the "down-to-earth" style, I felt that the technical standards when danced by professionals should be raised to a much higher level than when these movements are danced in their original forms by the peasants.

'I couldn't agree more', he said, 'that is how I work with my dancers'.

His encouraging words gave me further confidence to mention to him a major problem of mine that was especially sensitive in communist countries from the point of view of socialist ideology.

Although one part of the profession seemed to agree with my approach, many of the Hungarian folk dance experts disagreed with my ideas. They were worried about a so-called "balletification" of the authentic style. After a short time of thinking he said: 'I guess this kind of problem is not unique but – judging from the short demonstration I have just seen of your work – I believe your approach is definitely artistic and professional. Of course, one should see much more in order to give you a proper valuation. My advice to you is to continue on your chosen path because it seems to me to be the right one. Don't lose your enthusiasm; just carry on creating the rest with the same principles. Fight for your ideas if you must.' and with an impish wink he added 'That's what I do'.

So, I continued to teach my youngsters. Besides the Hungarian peasant style I also started to work on some of the ethnic ones – like the Romanian and the Hungarian Gypsy styles. With a colleague of mine (also a leading dancer from my theatre), we planned to start a small company formed from my best senior students and from some young professional dancers. I choreographed a one-act character ballet for them based on a folk-ballad.

We were just a few days away from the opening night and rehearsing feverishly in the late evening when, suddenly and brutally, politics and history interrupted us. We heard heavy gunfire, hand-grenade explosions, "Molotov-cocktails" and machine-gun fire. The sky became red from the flames of burning buildings. This was the first night of the Hungarian uprising against the Communist regime and the Russian occupation in October 1956 when the street fights started in earnest. From our rehearsal, which sadly proved to be the last activity of this seedling company, we could hardly get home safely. All public transport stopped except for the Russian tanks and Hungarian ambulance cars that continuously criss-crossed the capital sounding their deafening sirens. By that time street fights had claimed a lot of lives as well as injuring people.

For months to come normal life did not exist in Hungary. Except for fighting, looting on the streets and burying the dead – Russians as well as Hungarians – nothing else happened. There was a rumour that some of the minefields on Hungary's western border were temporarily cleared. So, many thousands of Hungarians (amongst them my scientist husband and I) risked an escape from this Hell to the Free World. We were lucky to be amongst the few hundreds who were given refuge, as well as the chance to settle, in England.

Our existence in our newly adoptive country depended on immediate work. Naturally, I started to look for work in my profession after arrival.

Slowly But Surely

The curiosity and welcome towards my work as a teacher of classical ballet and character dancing by the majority of the British dance-teaching profession has been greatly touching and overwhelming. After my arrival from Hungary some of the vocational schools and dance organisations showed interest in my work. In a relatively short time I was asked to give a few introductory classes and lectures in both classical ballet and character. Soon I received further invitations to teach for longer periods, like a course, especially in the field of character studies.

I was also approached by various British dance organisations (Royal Academy of Dancing, as well as the Imperial Society of Teachers of Dancing, and the British Ballet Organization) to give lecture-demonstrations at their Refresher Courses, Assembly Weeks, and Easter and Summer Courses for teachers and scholarship students.

Just before I left Hungary (1955–56) I had improved and expanded my character system to include a few more national styles (Romanian Peasant, Russian, Hungarian Court, Hungarian Gypsy, Polish and Georgian). I based this further work on the same ideas that I used initially when creating my system for teaching the Hungarian peasant style. So, by the time I was asked to teach my character system by some vocational schools on their regular timetables, I was prepared and ready.

Quite a few teachers, trainee teachers and some freelance professional dancers wished to study both classical ballet and character dancing with me. Several, who had their own private studios (Kathleen Crofton, Audrey DeVos, Helen Wingrave, Nesta Brooking, the Cone-Ripman school) organised some special courses and private lessons for me to teach. As far as the character studies were concerned, I was especially pleased to see that most of those attending were interested not only in just learning some East-European dance-styles and a few authentic dances from me, but they wanted to study my character dance system in detail. They seemed to understand and value the ideas behind the structure as well as the build up within each class.

My extended teaching plan for the seven contrasting styles became even more essential when I was invited onto the faculty of the Royal Academy's Teacher Training Course as a regular character teacher. I worked out a timetable to study five styles only during the three years of their course. I believed that doing less, but with the right quality, was better and safer than proceeding in a hurry. Also, knowing that the majority of these trainee teachers would go on to teach the younger and non-vocational pupils, I was convinced that the Gypsy and Georgian studies might be too sophisticated for their future needs.

As a rule, during the first year students studied the Hungarian peasant and the Romanian styles, each for one and a half terms. This way they had enough time not only to learn the steps and style, but also to get rid of inhibitions and dance in a manner completely different from their usual classical and refined way. They had to change their "restrained" attitude and become more extrovert, down-to-earth, with real flesh and blood characters in their dancing. Once "the ice was broken", one could continue faster and they picked up the other styles much more easily. The students learned to recognise what makes one style so different from the others; how a head-movement, a stance, the use of a hand, a prop or a different emphasis of a specific movement, dramatically changes the style. In the next year we worked on the Russian, Polish and the Hungarian court, each style for one term. During these two years the lessons were organised in such a way that I gave plenty of opportunities for each student to teach one another and, if needed, to correct faults by precise movement-analysis.

In the third year we spent our time doing a full recap of the total material they had learnt during the previous six terms. As a reminder, I gave one class of each style learnt previously. From then on they had to teach one another a more complex teaching practice:- building up to a longer étude or a whole class in a given style. I was delighted to see that my principle ideas – to study each style in a block separately – brought the required results, and was satisfied that by the time the students gained their diplomas they had the right idea about this subject matter, namely: what to teach and how. They were aware that the right structure of a character class is a necessity in order to avoid causing injuries and overdeveloped muscles.

I felt that it was important that not only the students of the Royal Academy Teacher Training Course, but all my character dance students, should understand why I was teaching them those specific styles. One obvious reason was that these were the national styles I had had the chance to study in detail. Also, I knew that in Britain, as well as in Commonwealth countries, many schools included in their timetable Irish, Scottish and Spanish dancing taught by experts. The East European styles that I was able to offer were entirely different. Adding these to the existing ones nicely complemented the students' technical and stylistic knowledge, widening their artistic horizons.

In addition, teaching the Hungarian, Russian and the Romanian peasant styles proved to be very useful in general dance studies. In these styles – apart from the interesting and unusual rhythms, time signatures and usage of cross-rhythms and unusual musical phrasing – students have to learn to dance together as a group in given floor patterns. They must relate to each other's movements while keeping distances, holding on to each other in all possible versions of joined hands – in simple circles, concentrically moving ones, in couples, semi-circles, straight lines, horse-shoes or in long chains of snake-like patterns.

From the point of view of dance students' general technique there is another great advantage in studying some of these folklore styles. Practising some diagonal turns, *pirouettes* and *tours en l'air* with the hands kept on the hips, or arms held in low diagonal, or *à la seconde* (as well as wearing boots, full skirts, hats, necklaces, and so on) is actually harder to do than their classical counterparts. Without boots, heavy skirts, head-dress, etc., as well as with the use of the helpful *port de bras*, the dancers are bound to perform with greater speed when it comes to executing these movements in their classical ballet versions. Likewise, when wearing character boots or shoes in the high jumps, the male dancer's landing might be noisier then when wearing ballet slippers, unless the dancer learns to do it with perfect control of his body alignment and foot and knee control when landing in a *fondu*. More control to overcome a noisy landing in boots or shoes will improve their landing technique in general.

Teaching the Polish and Hungarian court styles is essential when preparing vocational students to join any company that performs the traditional classical *repertoire*, as most of these include character dances of those styles. I was convinced then – and am even more certain about it six decades later – that all of the above mentioned material could and should be included in the regular timetable of all dance-schools. Amateur students can benefit and enjoy these studies, provided they are given the chance to study them regularly, in well-constructed classes given by experts. There are so many of these youngsters whose bodies are unsuitable for professional work, but who have the right spirit, musicality, intelligence and love of dancing. To be able to dance at their school-performances, and in many other amateur-shows, will give them creative and artistic fulfilment. At the same time their studies and performances will also inform their appreciation for the art of dance. As these are the future "dance audience", it is important for the advancement of our art form that their taste should demand refinement and subtlety in character dances on the professional stage.

So, having a fair amount of knowledge about these styles, I was able to create separate and specific barre exercises and centre études accordingly. In the case of the Russian style I didn't need to "create" anything as there was an existing Russian character dance system. This was formulated by the principal character dancer and teacher of the St. Petersburg company and school, Andrei Lopokov. I was lucky to study this in detail. This was the only existing character dance system but it was not meant to be only for Russian dancing. These technically-testing, rich barre exercises and centre études were mixed from a stylistic point of view.

As the essence of my character system was to teach the various styles separately and in one block, I picked out from Lopokov's system only those exercises, steps and études that were typically Russian. I also took great care that these demanding exercises should be taught alternating the supporting leg often, and that any contractions of the calf and thigh muscles should be followed by relaxing movements, and that the breathing should always be controlled.

The Georgian and Gypsy styles I taught only to professional dancers and those teachers who were teaching mature and vocational students.

During the following decades while regularly teaching trainee teachers – at the Royal Academy and later for the Royal Ballet School's Teacher Training Course – I developed another important "routine". Before I started to teach a certain style I always gave these trainee teachers a lecture. This contained a short historical and cultural background of the country whose dance style we were going to study, as well as a description of some of the typical national costumes, head-dresses, footwear and jewellery – often showing them photos and drawings – as these determine greatly the movements. It goes without saying that I called their attention to the importance of using the right music. I insisted they make detailed notes about the essence of these lectures.

I hoped that they would keep these records and refer to them from time to time. I thought that these notes might help these young teachers – as well as their future students – to feel more at ease when trying to "slip under the skin" of those unknown people, and their habits, feelings and behaviour, whose dances they performed and music they used. I warned them that when, in the future, they wish to teach character dancing and follow the structure of my system they would have to progress slowly. In the first stages this will seem to bring much slower results then conveying to their students just a few dances without proper preparations. However, in the long run, to go slower with thorough preparation will bring far better results, and real quality in their work. At the same time they might save their students from unnecessary injuries. I wished to call their attention to how important in our profession this subject matter is, and accordingly, to feel some responsibility when teaching it. I wanted them to understand how much depends on we teachers and our good work, so that future generations of audiences, critics, teachers, dancers and choreographers will have greater refinement and sensitivity towards the differing character styles.

I was greatly helped in this "mission" of mine by the fact that from time to time, the Royal Academy of Dancing and the Imperial Society of Teachers of Dancing commissioned me to choreograph some character dances, which I taught to members and examiners. Some of these dances were added to the Royal Academy's existing syllabi, so they were taught all over the world. I choreographed them in such a way that, apart from the required style, each had to express moods, human feelings, situations and sometimes even little stories. In this way the short dances became more popular with the students and I could emphasise that character dancing can be much more than just dancing the right steps with the required national flavour.

When I was devising these dances, I also considered that they were meant to suit both vocational students and a vast number of dance pupils all over the world with differing backgrounds and standards. They were received with interest and learnt with enthusiasm; a very satisfying experience for me.

At the same time I couldn't help worrying that teaching these dances for examiners and teachers at some of these vast gatherings could become a very superficial exercise. Many had to learn these dances in a short time and in very overcrowded classes. A number grasped the steps and rhythms remarkably fast. Still, I hardly had a chance to convey those personal corrections so important for the clarity of the appropriate style. It also worried me that without the beneficial style-preparing barre exercises and études in the centre – underpinning the technique and style of the matching dances – they might not be able to do justice to the quality of their teaching.

It was consoling to hear that everyone realised this danger, and numerous and continuous refresher courses were organised immediately afterwards. On most of these courses, the participants asked particularly to be taught the specifically related barre-exercises and études as well as the dances. For these reasons colleagues from Canada, New Zealand, Australia and South Africa arranged to have private lessons with me, as they were unable to stay in London for a longer time.

The directors of the RAD asked me to include these dances in the schedule of the Teacher Training Course. One day as I was teaching trainee teachers, Dame Margot Fonteyn, as the president of the RAD, visited us. She had heard about my character work from both the RAD and the Royal Ballet School where I was also teaching my system regularly. Dame Margot became interested and asked me to show her the dances I had devised for the RAD. So, the trainee teachers danced them for her and she seemed to like what she saw. Afterwards she asked me a lot of questions regarding my character work. I explained to her my principle ideas about character teaching, and mentioned also my worries in connection with the present project. Dame Margot liked my ideas concerning the systematic and structured teaching of the subject, but made me understand how complicated it might be to change all syllabi in such a widely extended organisation. However, she promised to bear my ideas in mind and to help to bring them to realisation gradually in the future.

Indeed, later on her promise started to come to realisation. Keith Lester, the director of the RAD's Teacher Training Course, was working on a completely new syllabus called The Dance Education Syllabus Levels I, II & III. He asked me to share in this work by devising the Character part of it. As he knew my system well and agreed with it entirely, he wanted me to base this syllabus on the structure of my system, complete with some of the specific and related barre-exercises and études that lead up to the dances. My collaborator, Mavis Barr, who worked with me ever since I started teaching in England, specially arranged the music for this syllabus from original folk songs. I chose the Russian style for Level I; the Hungarian for Level II; and the Romanian for Level III. The syllabus and music were published by the RAD in 1975.

In the meantime the Royal Ballet School also started a Teacher Training Course. Dame Ninette de Valois invited me to teach my system on this course as well.

Let Your Hair Down

∞∞

Teaching my character system at the Royal Ballet School was one of the most exciting challenges that I had been given so far in my newly adopted country. In 1961 Dame Ninette de Valois asked me to teach students from the Upper School. At first I taught those national styles that students would always need when they join a ballet company: Polish, Hungarian Court and Russian, and later I added to the curriculum Gypsy and Georgian dancing.

At the beginning, in spite of the perfectly disciplined and polite behaviour of the youngsters, I was aware of a slight trace of suspicion lingering in the atmosphere and that the majority were rather reserved. I wasn't quite sure why. Did they resent the subject matter I was teaching them? Perhaps they were too inhibited to step out of their formal and familiar surroundings whilst slipping under the skin of strange, extrovert characters who live in circumstances they don't know. Probably they were afraid that by practising the flamboyant and energetic movements that most styles demand, they might gain overdeveloped muscles and/or risk injury.

I hoped that I guessed correctly the causes of their aloofness, because I remembered only too well from my own student days when all my schoolmates and I had similar problems. If I wanted to achieve good results with these students, I'd have to win them over in the shortest possible time. The only way to do that was to show them that their worries were unwarranted.

As my classes followed the structure and build up of classical ballet practice, the students soon felt themselves on familiar ground and began to trust my system. As a result they danced in a relaxed manner that, in turn, prevented them from developing heavy-looking muscles as well as becoming easily prone to injuries. In such an atmosphere I was able to encourage them to express a variety of emotions, moods and situations through their movements. They seemed to welcome this challenge just as much as competing with each other on technical merit. Gradually we got to the point where they danced without inhibition and, as the idiom says, they "let their hair down".

I kept emphasising that in character dancing: 'the correct execution of the steps of a specific character style and technical mastery is absolutely necessary, but it is not enough. These are only the foundation stones for an artistic performance. To give purpose and meaning to these movements as well as style and technique is the "magic" we must strive for always. However, one cannot fulfil this goal without having some knowledge about the historic and cultural background of the people whose dancing one studies. So, before we start on a specific style, as well as during our work, I will always give you some background information.'

After a while I felt that the graduate class was making good progress and was ready to start on Hungarian Gypsy dancing. As an introduction, I explained not only the lifestyle and history of the Gypsies living in Hungary but I drew attention to certain special facts.

'In this style the girls dance with a specific alignment of the body, moving their head and torso in a rather unusual way and completely differently from the one we have in classical ballet practice. This extraordinary co-ordination is one of the determining factors in the manner of their dancing; the unusually synchronised movements are a natural consequence of the Gypsy girls' free flowing hairstyle. It is part of their identity, like the jewellery they are wearing or the music they play. Consequently, when studying these movements, the dancers must practise with similar hairdos. In this way the unusual movements will become natural instead of an affectation.'

Needless to say, classical ballet-trained students, used to dancing with a tidily arranged knot that won't interfere with any movement, find it strange to dance with disorganised hair, specifically when turning or jumping. Without practising and learning the technique of how to cope with trailing long hair when dancing, it becomes quite a nuisance and ends up in a mess. 'From now on in your character lessons please let your hair down, meaning it in both the practical and the figurative sense.'

These girls always worked in their character classes with enthusiasm and showed genuine ambition to excel in them. So, I was most surprised when they arrived for the next lesson out of breath and late and, worse, their hair was arranged in a tidy bun!

'What is the meaning of all this?' I asked disappointedly. 'I hope you have a proper excuse for such behaviour but I can't listen to it now! You've already lost precious minutes and you are going to lose even more, as you can't start your Gypsy dancing unless you have the proper hairdo. So, get on with it and let it down quickly'. They rushed towards the classroom door in order to get to their dressing rooms, but I impatiently stopped them: 'No, no, no! Please don't waste further time by running backwards and forwards. Do it here and now!'

The students looked upset and as if they wanted to tell me something but, for some reason or another, they didn't dare. Suddenly one of them, a girl from Iceland, while undoing her rich blonde bun said timidly: 'I am so sorry Madame Fay but it's all my fault. We let down our hair as you asked and were on our way in time for class.' By that time she loosened her hair that covered literally almost the whole of her slight figure. I have never ever seen in my life such beautiful, immensely long and golden tresses (except in Debussy's opera *Pelléas et Mélisande,* and that, of course, was a wig!).

'As we were on our way to the classroom I was fooling around a bit using my hair as the seven veils of Salome,' she continued while illustrating her words with a couple of exaggerated Gypsy-ish images to which she purposely added some comical edge. With a few movements she created an immensely funny parody – it looked to me like a "send up" of a night club dancer – making a good use of the contradiction between her angelic looks and the provocatively sensual movements. 'We were coming along the corridor giggling,' she continued with a guilty expression on her face, 'when we met Miss Edwards. She looked a bit shocked and asked: 'have you girls finished for the day?' When we told her that we are actually on our way to character class she became very cross with us and said: 'How dare you go to Madame Fay's class without your obligatory hairstyle! This is the most disrespectful behaviour towards your teacher!'

'But, Miss Edwards …' we tried to explain, but she cut us short saying firmly: 'No buts! Unless you redo your hair immediately, you'll go nowhere but to the director's office!' She was very angry and watched us while we went back to our dressing room to do up our hair into buns.

By that time the rest of the class could hardly control their chuckling. I found it hard to keep a straight face and likewise my pianist, Mavis Barre. Knowing how patient and understanding my friend Winifred Edwards has always been towards young dancers, and how sincere a supporter she has been of my work ever since I started to teach in Britain, I understood why she became outraged on my behalf and wanted to "shield my image". Of course, she didn't know what the real reason was for the girls "letting their hair down".

The whole situation reminded me more of a farce than a serious "disciplinary matter" in a vocational school. Besides, I was secretly also very much taken by this girl's little performance. It was a brilliant characterisation, giving a spontaneous and "meaningful" quality for character movements.

Later I explained the situation to dear Winifred and we also had a good giggle!

Style Awareness

After my first year with the students of the Royal Ballet Upper School, I was asked to teach my character system also to 5th form pupils of the Lower School. Every Saturday morning the school bus brought these youngsters from White Lodge to the Upper School's studios. I was delighted by this new task, as my opinion always was that vocational students should start studying character dancing as early as possible.

I knew that these students had already learnt some Irish, Scottish and Morris dancing, so I aimed to widen their knowledge in the field of character dancing by introducing other differing national styles that were in absolute contrast to those they already knew. For the first one and a half terms I taught them Romanian dancing and in the following one and a half terms Hungarian peasant style. At the same time – with the help of the corresponding barre exercises and études in the centre – I hoped to improve their stamina and technical skills without overstraining their vulnerable young bodies.

Besides these important goals, I gave myself an even more significant one. Apart from teaching these youngsters the steps of the national style in question together with the correct arm and body movements, I hoped to kindle in them a virtue that I call "style awareness" which, combined with good taste, I believe every young dancer should develop.

I still am convinced that, apart from character studies, in the general upbringing of young professional dancers one should cultivate a sensitivity that is geared to recognise the nuances in movements that might determine the various styles. Bringing this useful quality to the fore does play an essential role in every dancer's future professional life. Whether as dancers in a company or freelance professionals, they will have to learn and perform numerous classical and modern ballets as well as contemporary pieces of an ever-widening dance-repertoire that includes many strongly differing styles.

These works were choreographed in the different periods of dance history and have typical signs of the times in which they're composed and performed. Let's call this the general period style (classical, romantic, etc.) created by choreographers who all have their own personal style stamped on their work: the creator's individual style.[13] When soloists learn roles that were previously created for some famous personality, they should sense and recognise those stylistic elements that come from the choreographer, those that a previous interpretative artist might have added, and those which might stem from répétiteurs' personalities. Good taste, knowledge and style awareness will help a dancer to pick and choose correctly those elements which should be saved, while adding their own individual interpretation when re-creating a given role. This is the interpreter's personal style.[14]

When musicians, singers and actors are nurtured, the enhancement of style awareness and the differentiation of these three elements (general period style, creator's individual style, and interpreter's personal style) are taken quite seriously. As a result the majority of audiences have become more aware of the importance of a stylish interpretation and expect such from the artists.

I felt that character dance studies, by their very nature, are an extremely good vehicle to achieve this goal. In these classes one influences in a young dancer a specific "vision" and "hearing". They can learn to look out for those slight movement elements that might determine a certain style, and how to hear – in spite of the silence of movement – a specifically characterising rhythm and emphasis. In this way they are likely to develop the necessary sensitivity and capability to quickly notice and absorb the style-determining elements.

I explained to them: 'We are living in an age when almost every choreographer (whether of classical ballet or contemporary dance) has a particular style and technique. Today, most professional companies have a very mixed repertoire and the dancers must adapt technique and style accordingly. It is impossible to teach you, and for you to learn, all these variants during a few years of study at a vocational school.

---

[13] Bournonville, Petipa, Balanchine, Ashton, Tudor, MacMillan, van Manen, Graham, Bruce, Cunningham, etc.
[14] Pavlova, Nijinsky, Ulanova, Fonteyn, Nureyev, Guillem, Graham, Forsythe, etc.

However, it is possible for you to achieve a generally strong technique that enables you to cope with all sorts of requirements and, at the same time, to develop refined style awareness'.

During lessons I frequently called students' attention to the small details of a movement (of stance, expression, rhythm, and dynamic) which define a style and delineate it from others. I tried to make them understand that certain basic movements (like *pas de basque*, pivot-turns, *pas marché, cabrioles, ballonnés, temps levé sautés*) are executed in numerous different ways according to the national character the dancer is representing.

'A good character dancer's goal is to make sure that when executing any steps from any style they are danced not only with precision and perfect technical skill, but also with the most sensitive stylistic interpretation. The combination of all these elements can be learnt by any willing and systematically taught vocational student and will produce satisfying results on stage.

'Additionally, some interpretation will contain a unique quality that cannot be learnt but is triggered by an artist's personality. When a dancer allows their inner-self to rise to the surface and shine through the required characterisation, this is what you call a magical performance. In order to achieve this you shouldn't hold back anything when practising. Then, perhaps, one day you also will be able to give magical interpretations.'

It didn't take these junior students too long to drop their slightly shy attitudes. They took to character classes like "ducks to water" with enthusiastic eagerness that, in turn, resulted in remarkable progress.

It was a great comfort to me to see that the ideas from which my character system was built were bringing good results. It was worthwhile being patient and allowing plenty of time to study each national style separately in a block, and that during this period each lesson was based on a corresponding barre and centre practice. Studying in this manner was a way of avoiding injuries and, at the same time, the awareness about style became second nature. Students picked up the differing styles of character studies much faster, so we needed only one term to learn a new style. All this proved that time invested during early studies pays good dividends later on.

Who Cares What The Critics Say?

After I had been teaching at the Royal Ballet School for a while, Ursula Morton, then Associate Director of the school, took quite an interest in my character system. She frequently came to watch the classes. One Saturday, at the beginning of a summer term, after she had seen several classes in succession she told me:

'The progress of the students in the character studies is impressive! I've informed Dame Ninette about this and she seemed to be really interested. She's returning from her present work in Turkey at about half term and I am sure that she'll want to see this for herself. If she finds it as pleasing as I do – as I think she might – her intention is to show these achievements at the end of the school year in the School Performance at Covent Garden. If you agree with this idea, you'd better start the preparations for that event.'

Needless to say I did agree and was very pleased. After all, from the time I started to teach my character system to these students, my most important goal was to make them ready for the stage; to be able to perform the subject with clarity, skill, maturity, sensitivity and quality. So, this event was going to be the "proof of the pudding".

At the same time the task also terrified me; trying to do justice to the work of so many students at all ages and levels (all in all 146 young dancers). The attitude of most students towards character work was very good and they were industrious and enthusiastic but, depending which classes they belonged to, their skill, maturity, as well as their talents were naturally at different levels. It wasn't a simple task for me to find a suitable frame – without compromising technical and artistic standards – in which all the students would fit, get equal opportunities and could feel confident enough to be challenged to show their achievements at their personal best.

I thought that perhaps an étude-like choreography might just serve these goals. An étude can be constructed in such a way that, as in a class, each dancer has to execute the same tasks as their classmates. The chance to perform in public would be equal for all students; however the artistic delivery would be up to the talent of the individual student. I hoped that performing within a familiar class arrangement, with the familiar accompanist, and dancing amongst their own classmates would make the students feel confident enough not only to perform competently, but also to give all they had from a quality point of view. The students were also very happy with this news. They enthusiastically welcomed the possibility of showing in public the results of their character studies on one of the world's most illustrious stages. To have the school matinee held at the Royal Opera House wasn't taken for granted by the students at that time as, so far, it had happened only once before.

I decided to call the piece *"Etude Caractère"* and was going to set up the stage as a studio with the barre in a semicircle formation with the piano placed behind it on a pedestal. Mavis Barre – our regular pianist and my collaborator ever since I started to work in Britain – would accompany the dancers with music-arrangements she had composed previously for my character system and with some new ones created specifically for this occasion.

My plan was that each class would follow in succession and would represent one of the national styles they had studied, and it would be performed in a choreographic version in the pattern of their regular character classroom work.

I wanted to commence the *"Etude Caractère"* with the Junior School students. First they would do their barre exercises in Hungarian Peasant style, then continue in the centre with steps and *enchaînements* that would culminate in a short choreography of a Csárdás danced in a circle (called "karikázó" in Hungarian). The next group, the youngest in the Upper School, would follow them with the Polish style barre and centre work that would conclude in a performance of a specially choreographed Mazurka. This would be followed by the class, which represented the Russian style and that would reach its climax in a Russian dance. Afterwards we would see those students who demonstrate the Hungarian

Gypsy style dancing their barre and centre exercises and finishing it with Gypsy dancing. The Georgian style barre and centre *enchaînements* – represented by the graduate students with their Georgian Gliding Dance – would bring the final curtain down on the whole presentation. That was the plan and, of course, in order to bring it to realisation in just one term, there was a lot of work involved for all of us.

It was obvious that by teaching character systematically and consistently, the students' style awareness was growing gradually from strength to strength. However, there was an even more important question to be answered. It troubled me that my theory – that once a student achieved a high level of sensitivity for differentiating between various styles it would help them later in their professional life to pick up any other given style – was still not proven. I suddenly realised that an opportunity for putting this theory to the test had just arisen, and it occurred out of a specific circumstance.

There were five excellent oriental students in the Upper School. I asked them whether they had ever learnt any Chinese folklore. As their answer was in the negative I decided to choreograph for them a Chinese ribbon dance (a style they hadn't come across until now) based on folklore elements. To do this they had to learn the steps of my choreography and the style, as well as the technique of handling a six-yard-long ribbon and, on top of these difficulties, some mime elements to be delivered in the Chinese manner. For all this we had a very limited time – not more than professional dancers in similar situation. They picked up the style with ease and much faster than I ever hoped in my wildest imagination. I could be satisfied that my theory was proven, and added this piece to the rest of the *"Etude Caractère"*.

I knew that to get the right costumes for the many styles and dancers involved, and for the sake of only one occasion, would be impossibly expensive for the school. So I just settled for the students wearing their practice shoes and outfits that the school already possessed according to the specific style of their character studies.

The Hungarian, Polish and Russian class wore their regular character class outfits. The Georgian girls, in order to learn how to dance in long dress, had already been given full- length skirts for their Georgian class practice and, to assist with learning their elaborate hand and arm movements, they also had silk square scarves to practise with. The gypsy girls had their regular character skirts elongated with a six-inch frill. There were only the five oriental girls who were each given extraordinarily long silk ribbons attached to a stick, and a pair of silk pyjama trousers from the beginning of the rehearsals.

It was always on Saturday mornings that I worked with all the students and did detailed as well as "run-through" rehearsals. After a few weeks of feverish work by the dancers, musician, costume department and myself, Ursula Morton came to watch for the first time. Before we started the run-through she told us the news: in about two weeks' time Dame Ninette was to come and see the full rehearsal. By now all students had learnt their roles, but naturally there were still some "rough edges" that needed more rehearsal for refinements. Nevertheless, we were ready enough for an expert to see where we were heading.

At the beginning of the rehearsal our visitor seemed very pleased and she smiled encouragingly, but I couldn't help noticing that, as we commenced, she looked more and more nervous and her face became as white as a sheet with worry. I could see that the students also got wind of her nervousness and, in turn, they became nervous also. (Needless to say this unfortunate atmosphere didn't help their performing spirits!) The "run-through" lasted well over an hour and then I gave the performers a break. I was eager to hear from Miss Morton what she had to say and what was worrying her. With a panic-stricken expression she said: 'My dear Maria I can't believe what I just have seen!' Now it was my turn to get white in the face. 'What I mean is,' she continued, 'you have created a wonderful arrangement and at the same time you'll ruin it by trying to put on stage every student of each class! You can't mean this seriously, can you?'

'But of course I do. I might have misunderstood you but I took it for granted that this is just exactly what you'd expect me to do. As all the students of this school are studying character dancing with me, I thought they all should have the chance to perform on this occasion.'

'Well, we've never done that before. Many of them are not suitable to appear on the Covent Garden stage! What would the profession and the critics say? I am sure Ninette will never agree to this.'

To a certain point I understood her anxiousness. After all, in Madam's absence, she was responsible for the outcome of that year's School Matinee. Also, it was her suggestion to include the character-demonstration at this occasion. I tried to reassure Ursula (and myself) by saying: 'I can't deny that not all 146 students are exactly soloist material, however, I strongly believe that by the time of the performance all of them will reach the standards in character dance that we'd expect from vocational students. I thought that the whole idea was to give a chance to perform on stage to those students who might not have an ideal body to excel in classical ballet, but still have something valuable to offer to the audience. This gift – if they have it – might be discovered on such an occasion, but if they don't have it perhaps they shouldn't be here.'

'Believe me, it would be wiser if you'd start selecting the students and allow only for the best ones to rehearse from now on. You still have two weeks before her arrival.'

'If I may I would like to leave things as they are at the moment,' I carried on stubbornly, 'and give them all the benefit of the doubt, at least until we show the piece to Madam. There are quite a few amongst the students who are more withdrawn than the others, but that doesn't mean that by the time they get onto the stage they will be unable to perform the way we wish them to do. I hope that seven more weeks of polishing might just bring the expected results. Please, let's try, or rather, let them try.'

Although it was obvious that she wasn't really convinced either by my reasoning or my pleas, nevertheless she gave the impression that considering my arguments might be worthwhile. There was some resignation as well as a bit of teasing in her voice when she said: 'All right, all right my obstinate girl, go ahead and try to do it as you wish, but don't say you haven't been warned! I wash my hands of it.'

Having been warned by Ursula Morton I must confess that – in spite of the rapid progress of the students in the following two weeks – on the day of Madam's visit I was quite a bit nervous about the outcome. I prepared myself for the worst, just in case Ursula was right, but in front of the students I tried to look absolutely confident and encouraging. As the rehearsal progressed, and by watching Dame Ninette's facial expression while the students were doing their very best ,I had the "gut feeling" that after all, things might not turn out too badly.

When we reached the end of the rehearsal, for a moment or two there was a frightening silence, and I must admit that my heart was beating in my throat. Madam didn't say a word and as she turned her head away from the students – I hardly could believe what I was witnessing – she suddenly brushed away a few tears from her face while she smiled at me. Then, again quite composed, she turned to the students: 'I hope you are aware how lucky you are having Madame Fay as your teacher! I want you to know and appreciate the fact that Hungary's loss is Great Britain's gain'. I was speechless ... but at that point I knew that she obviously didn't mind at all having the "all student cast".

Even with wishful thinking I never would have dreamt about receiving such a generous compliment from such a senior figure of our profession! The students were also overwhelmed and burst into a big and happy ovation, clapping and shouting "bravo", looking in the direction of our pianist and myself. I could see that Ursula Morton was absolutely delighted and, I believe, as greatly relieved as I was. A few weeks later Madam was going to surpass her own generous gesture towards me even more. At the end of the school performance, from the stage of the Royal Opera House, she repeated to a packed house in front of the public, professionals and critics the same comment with additional complimentary sentences of appreciation about my work.

Amongst all artists who belong to any of the performing arts there is a well-known saying: 'Who cares what the profession and the critics might say about your performance or creation? After all, you are not performing and creating for them, but you do it for yourself and for the audience ...'

Of course this is true – or is it? I often tried to scrutinise this saying without a cynical attitude and came to the conclusion that it is only partially true. Indeed, perhaps one would like not to care (especially when getting some negative reaction from the press), but the truth is that in reality one does, at least I do ... especially when their write-ups are complimentary. So, I admit that I did care very much about what the press had to say after that performance. These reviews meant a lot to me for the rest of my professional life – as they did for the 146 students.

Dance Round The World

In my years of working in Western Europe I have been given quite a few chances to put to the test how to adapt my character system when teaching. I've also had plenty of opportunities to find out how to apply its benefit to different types of professional stage work.

There were occasions when I was asked to coach or polish the style of existing character dances in some of the traditional classical ballets, or to choreograph entirely new character dances within ballets or operas. I also experienced creating an entire character ballet for a classical company. Although all this work was interesting, challenging and highly satisfying, there were still some genres of the performing arts that I admired – like film and television – but, regrettably, had no chance to try out how my ideas about creating character dances would work for these media.

I didn't have to wait for too long before the first opportunity arose to try "my wings" in the fascinating field of the small screen. I was teaching regularly at Nesta Brooking's school. Besides her own students, Nesta welcomed some professional dancers and young teachers to participate in my character lessons. This practice proved to become very useful for her young students. Seeing the more sophisticated styles – like the Gypsy and Georgian – performed with the maturity of talented professionals helped and encouraged the youngsters to deliver strange movement-images in the manner of various ethnic groups about whose existence they hardly knew until they started to study with me. At the beginning of the character studies they were a bit timid but soon they "let their hair down" and improved remarkably.

Peggy van Praagh, then artistic director of the Australian Ballet, and a great friend of Nesta Brooking, visited the school and watched our character lesson. She seemed to be very impressed and asked if I would object to a television presenter, Fernau Hall, coming to watch. He was originally a student of Nesta's and later became dance critic of the *Daily Telegraph* and author of several dance books.

The outcome of this visit led to Nesta's students and I gaining our first job on British television (not to mention the beginning of a life-long friendship between Fernau and myself). Fernau taught me that when working in television one should think about dancing from the point of view of the camera. One has to understand the limitations as well as the possibilities the small screen can offer for dance. He gave the programme the title of *Dancing Round The World With Maria Fay*. It was broadcast on ITV's Schools' Programme Channel where we were given a 30-minute slot. The students of the Brooking school, led by some of those professional dancers who studied with them, danced arrangements that I choreographed specifically for the occasion, and this was interwoven with short interviews and "voice-overs".

By doing this programme I learnt important facts about television presentation. I started to understand how differently the choreographer and dancers must act and react when creating for the camera and not for the stage. (In the following decades all these experiences were of great help to me in creating my three videotapes.) I realised that to prepare a piece with meaningful and interesting movement-images and patterns, in harmony with the music and/or telling a story through dance, was not enough when dancing for the small screen.

I understood that the camera should not be looked on as just a useful invention for getting precise records of dance creations. Making a good visual film or videotape of dancing is an art form on its own and quite a sophisticated one. When composing for the camera a choreographer must also become the artistic co-ordinator between the director, dancers, conductor, composer, cameramen and editors and, when understanding all these artists' points of view, create accordingly.

This is not an easy task to achieve. However, this seems the only way to strike the right balance when choosing and mixing the close-ups, mid and wide shots; slow or fast motion, freezes, dissolves, black-outs and so on, in order to present our art form advantageously and tastefully to the wide-spread public of television. Without this knowledge it is pointless to do it at all.

The lessons I learnt from this experience became very useful and underpinned my work when the BBC engaged me from time to time for other choreographic tasks. I was asked to compose a mazurka in the ballroom scene of a production of Tolstoy's *Anna Karenina*; and a shepherd dance in the nativity-scene for Menotti's television opera *Amahl and the Night Visitors*. (I based my choreography on Yemenite folk dance traditions thinking that this style might be the closest to a folk dance in a barn 2000 years ago). In both productions I was, of course, working with professional dancers.

Following these activities several other television companies asked me to coach actors, actresses, singers and even extras who were to portray Hungarians, Gypsies, Russians, Romanians and the like, dancing on screen in the style of their portrayed nationality. All these jobs were very different from each other and, from the point of view of our art form, to very different standards. To try out my theory and the system of how to apply character dance successfully in several opera and drama productions on the small screen was fascinating.

Not long after these television productions I had a telephone call from a gentleman with an American accent saying, 'I am phoning from 20th Century Fox. We are shooting at the moment in Elstree Studios a feature film titled *The Inn of the Sixth Happiness* with Robert Donat and Ingrid Bergman. The film takes place in China and includes some dance. The director of the film is searching for a choreographer who is an expert in character dancing. Can you come and meet him tomorrow?'

Needless to say that at first it was flattering but also quite astonishing that one of the most famous production companies of the "big screen" was seriously interested in my work for the camera. However, lacking a bit of self-confidence, I had second thoughts and became suspicious about this call. It crossed my mind that perhaps it was a hoax, nothing more than a friend making a silly joke, or a teenage pupil having a bit of misplaced fun. If so, I thought, shall I just slam the receiver down or simply laugh it off? Perhaps one should react with some similarly childish prank pretending that one is a "good sport" and can take a joke no matter how stupid it was…

Luckily, I decided to ask the caller: 'Actually, how did you get my telephone number?' (My husband and I were at that time still in rented accommodation and our telephone was under the name of the property owner. This number was known only to close friends and professional institutions for which I had been working.)

'We turned to The Royal Ballet, BBC television and the Royal Academy of Dancing. They all suggested your name to us and gave your number.' This information was enough to convince me that, after all, this wasn't a hoax, so I went to the meeting the next day. I must admit I was pretty nervous about the possibility of becoming a choreographer for the big screen and, what's more, to work for one of the most distinguished of Hollywood's film companies. At the same time I was eagerly looking forward to the new challenges, experiences and lessons to be learnt.

I often heard from colleagues who had worked for big film companies that the artistic points of view of film directors – with few exceptions – usually clashed dramatically with those of choreographers and dancers. So, when I went to 20th Century Fox to meet the director of the film, I was curious to see what kind of experience was in store for me.

Besides a secretary taking notes, the film director, the producer and myself, there was a young Chinese man present at the meeting. His name was Mr Lee and I was told that he was a dancer from Hong Kong, but they didn't tell me why he was there. The director gave us a short synopsis of the film in which there was a scene where a Chinese aristocrat (played by Robert Donat) was dining with his European guests (Ingrid Bergman and Kurt Jurgens). During the meal the Mandarin gives orders for his concubines to entertain them with some dancing. 'This dance, of course, must be an absolutely authentic one.' said the director.

I was wondering what he meant by "absolutely authentic"? Was it traditional folk dance or the classical Peking Opera style? 'How long is that particular scene going to be?' I asked. The indisputable answer was 'Maximum two minutes.' Knowing that in the traditional classical Peking Opera Style a dance that lasts only two minutes doesn't exist as such, I thought he might mean a folk dance. But then this didn't make sense to me, as it was most unlikely that, in the given circumstances, concubines of a mandarin of refined taste would dance a folk dance. It seemed to me that the definition of an "absolutely authentic dance" just must be taken with quite a pinch of salt.

Probably what was needed in this film wasn't a real "authentic dance" but a choreography in which the movements were based on either classical Peking opera style or Chinese folklore. I wanted to make sure that my guess was correct, so I decided to ask some more leading questions. 'What have you in mind for accompaniment to the dance?' 'For rehearsals you'll be given some Chinese music recorded from an authentic score, and when we edit the film it will naturally be replaced with music from our composer'.

For the first time Mr Lee spoke, asking 'Is the composer Chinese?'. When the answer was 'No, he is an expert in film music.' he showed disappointment.

If there was no original score to be used as an accompaniment to the dance, I thought, it seemed to me obvious that the dance should be created in the same manner. I continued my "disguised inquisition" determinedly. 'How about costumes, footwear and hairstyles?' 'All will be designed in the traditional style including the most lavish wigs, hand-embroidered costumes, etc., etc. ... No expense will be spared.'

'How many concubines do you have in mind?' was my next question. 'About six and they all have to be dancers of either Chinese or Japanese origin. An audition has been organised for next week.' Indicating the young man from Hong Kong, I said quite innocently, 'Perhaps Mr Lee will be able to find good available Chinese dancers', but he seemed to be hurt and annoyed when I said this.

'Mr Lee was asked to be here' the producer quickly intervened, 'in a choreographer's capacity, as yourself.' Now it was my turn to be hurt. 'I don't understand,' I said, astonished. 'Then, apart from asking numerous questions, what is supposed to be my role here?' 'My dear lady', he said in a patronising yet somewhat arrogant manner, 'you are not the only choreographer we want to consult. We've already talked to several working in musical theatre, and we might be doing so after we have seen you. Then we'll decide to whom we'll offer the contract.'

'I'm trying to understand your point of view. Nevertheless, I find it an unusual and rather unpleasant situation in which you place Mr Lee and myself. Two choreographers being consulted in front of each other seems to me as though we were expected to bid or compete for the contract'. I couldn't, and wouldn't, hide my sarcasm. 'How do you want us to fight this kind of artistic duel?'

They either didn't seem to notice or mind my sarcasm, or might have taken it for granted that this kind of fighting arena was the way one does business in the world of the great American film companies. However, I didn't feel any inclination to become part of it. 'I am afraid I have to leave you to further consultation with Mr Lee in my absence,' I said while looking at my watch, 'as I am due to teach in half-an-hour.' 'Sure, sure, but would you at least give us just some indication how you would go about choreographing this dance?' the director said.

'Well, to put it in a nutshell: I think what you need is a short, purpose-made choreography based on authentic elements in the Chinese classical style, charming, feminine and spectacular, that would aim to complement rather then interrupt the action of this scene. Forgive me, but now I must dash.' 'Sure, sure,' said the director again and was quite amicable while shaking hands and saying 'it was nice to meet you'. I was convinced that I'd never hear from them. However, the same evening I had a telephone call from the director: 'When you told me how you'd choreograph for us in the given scene and situation, you won my trust. You are the right person for us.' I was offered the contract.

The next day the director and I had a brief talk. We agreed that I'd base my choreography on a Manchurian custom whereby girls dance with two burning candles each. The idea delighted the director because this tradition wasn't so much known in the western world, and also because he saw an interesting possibility for using specific lighting effects when following the intricate movements of the 12 lit candles. After this meeting I signed the contract (a rather generous one), and I thought that my troubles and surprises were over. Not a bit of it! It was only the tip of the iceberg.

At the time (in the sixties) there were just a few professional dancers of Chinese or Japanese origin in London. 20th Century Fox contacted them but immediately turned them down, as these dancers asked for fees a bit above the Equity minimum. I had to audition and choose girls from Chinese students and "extras" who hardly had any dancing experience! In order to achieve fairly good results I had to rehearse these amateurs over six weeks (with professionals that would have taken a maximum of 2 weeks, and surely with better artistic results.) While saving the pennies we lost the pounds.

We were told that we'd get specially-made red candles with hand-painted gold characters on them that were guaranteed not to blow out. As they cost a small fortune, we'd have them only on the day of shooting. Until then we had to rehearse with ordinary ones. So I used the cheapest candles one could get at Woolworths, and made sure that the girls learnt how to keep these ordinary candles burning while they danced. At the same time I warned the props department not to make the candles longer then 10 to 15 centimetres, as dancing with longer ones might prove impossible without the flame catching some part of the dancers' costume or wig.

On the day of shooting we received the purpose-made candles. They were beautiful but, alas, kept blowing out constantly during the dance and were 24 cm long! However, we tried our best until one girl's elaborate wig and another's hand-embroidered, pure silk costume went up in flames but, luckily, they weren't harmed. However, it wasn't until three days later (after lots of money was spent on a new costume and wig, and new candles of the correct size) that all this was sorted out, and we could start shooting without further distractions.

It was reassuring that the director thought highly of the dance and was painstakingly anxious about special lighting effects, which I agreed with, and shooting angles – some of which I didn't agree with, but I couldn't make him change them.

Most of this didn't matter at all. The film turned out to be much too long, and it was decided that about 45 minutes had to be cut. Needless to say, the dance was one of the sacrificial lambs. There remained only a few glimpses of it in the final version.

Which One is Which?

∽∼∾

In the early 1960s, John Field, the artistic director of the touring company of the Royal Ballet (now Birmingham Royal Ballet), visited the Royal Ballet School to watch my Polish character class. Afterwards he asked me whether I would consider "revitalising" the Mazurka and the Csárdás in his company's *Coppélia*.

'It seems that as the years pass by, with the numerous rehearsals and performances of the same production, the character dances keep losing their style and especially their freshness, they are a bit dusty and moth-eaten ... Would you polish them for us?' I went to watch their next rehearsal.

Naturally, the choreography of both dances was – as far as we know them today – more or less the Saint-Léon/Petipa version. I found that, in the delivery of the well known steps and *port de bras* of the Mazurka, the dancers needed not only a bit of "polishing" and "revitalising" but some style studies as well. The style of the so-called Csárdás – it was actually much more in the style of a palotás (Hungarian Court dancing) than a folkloric csárdás – needed even more sophisticated corrections, although the dancers were not at all lacking in performing skills. They did their best and performed both dances with the most generous smiles you could ask for, and "stamped their feet, clicked their heels, clapped their hands and looked jolly".

However, in my eyes the main cause for worry lay in there being hardly any differentiation between the two national styles. Watching them danced in rehearsal, without the revealing stage costumes, one would hardly recognise which dance was supposed to be the Hungarian and which the Polish (except for the music, time signature and the well-known mazurka step). As there are some basic steps in both of these choreographies that are almost identical this was a quite understandable error and, it is only fair to say, I have witnessed this symptom occur in quite a number of other honourable companies.

I knew that the company could offer me only a very limited number of rehearsals in their overloaded schedule. I had to find a method that could convey to the dancers in a fast and effective way the dominant characteristics of the two different styles, and that the secret of the right presentation lay in the manner and quality of performance.

I guessed that everybody expected me to conduct a few "spring cleaning rehearsals"; that would have been the usual practice (breaking up the choreography into small units and making detailed corrections in the first bit; repeating this procedure with the next bit; and so on …). In this way the dancers would have been given a large amount of corrections squashed into a short period of time. Their movements would have been corrected – but I was afraid that this procedure wouldn't give the dancers a chance to understand the root of the problem. As a result the delivery of the dances would still be just an empty, meaningless and routine performance. I explained all this to John Field and added, 'This is a more sophisticated matter then it seems at a first glance. In order to avoid a superficial solution I have to set up the rehearsals in an unorthodox way.'

For my first rehearsal I asked for double length rehearsal time and to their surprise and slight resentment I called both the Csárdás and the Mazurka groups to appear together.

'The aim of our rehearsals' I explained, 'is to bring more life and style into the two national dances of this ballet. In order to get good results in a short time, we must clarify some of the specific historical background of both the Polish and Hungarian nations. Knowing more about them will throw a light on the reasons why both nations' dance-cultures are easily confused, and will help you to deliver a more sensitive and delineated interpretation of both styles.

'Between the 14th and 17th century the Poles and the Hungarians often chose to share their kings and ruling princes. Sometimes the monarch was Polish and at other times he was Hungarian. Most of the time this political arrangement worked surprisingly well, as both nations were allowed to keep their national autonomy, language and culture. To keep this political relationship a friendly one was perhaps greatly helped by the circumstance that, in both countries, the majority of the population practised the same Roman Catholic religion.

'As the bonds between the two nations were amicable it was a natural and harmless process that the nobility and the intelligentsia on both sides benignly influenced each other's cultural life. This influence was noticeable in both countries' architecture (churches and country mansions), and anything to do with the formal and aristocratic life including etiquette, entertainment, sports, fashion, clothing, music and dancing. This cultural influence, however, hardly touched the life of the majority of the population in either country, so it didn't much influence the folklore.

'Before the 19th century in European civilisation composers and dancing masters seldom built their creations on folk traditions. Therefore the previous centuries' dancing masters – whose main occupation was to teach the members of the nobility some decent ballroom dancing – didn't find it too important to sort out those details that distinguished the two styles from each other. Most of them just aimed to satisfy the demands and taste of their noble employers. As long as their pupils were able to execute the steps, and they were spectacular enough, fitting to the given music and the set time signature (3/4 in the case of the mazurka and 2/4 or 4/4 in the "csárdás-called" palotás) they seemed satisfied. This is why some basic steps (like the *pas de bourrée*, *cabrioles*, stamp and clap, breaking step) and *port de bras* are often presented more or less in the same way in both styles.

'When dancers of today portray the nobles of these two nations – especially when the dances of both countries are within the same ballet as in *Coppélia* or in *Swan Lake* – they should emphasise in their performance the subtle but style-determining movements to the maximum, and minimise as much as possible the similarities.

'In *Coppélia* the whole action takes place in a small Silesian village lying on the border between Hungary and Poland. The population is made up of Hungarian and Polish villagers. These country folk at special occasions would dance both the mazurka and the csárdás, but naturally these should never be performed in the nobility's manner but rather in a folkloric style.

'This means that the quality of the movements in both dances must be different, less formal in manner and, in the Mazurka's case, should be danced at a noticeably faster speed. (Delibes' music supports – if not demands – these qualities.) Also, the bond between the two sexes is expressed in a more natural and freer manner. So apart from the "sorting out procedure", you must add all these qualities to your performance. However, in the case of the Csárdás, the situation will be a bit more complicated, as the traditional choreography is much closer to a palotás than a csárdás.

'For the time being, forget the actual choreography and please go to the barre.' Again, there was surprise and some indignation amongst the dancers, but I pretended not to notice. I taught them a Hungarian barre exercise in the palotás style that corresponded with the style of the music of Delibes, and with the specific steps that were used in the Csárdás of *Coppélia*.

I called the dancers' attention to how a slight change of stance, a rhythmical delay (rubato) of an arm movement in a *port de bras*, an anticipation of a head movement, a slight dragging of a leg, the use of a prolonged *épaulement*, or an almost belated and snappy stamp of the foot, click of the heels, or a clap, could entirely change the style of a certain movement. I asked the rehearsal pianist to accompany these barre exercises with a variety of authentic folk music that helped to underpin these points. Then we continued with a centre practice making use of the typical and distinctive Hungarian accents they had just practised in the barre work.

After this kind of intellectual, physical and musical preparation, I asked the pianist to play Delibes' music and for the dancers to perform the given Csárdás. It seemed quite natural for them to dance it with the correct stylistic accents and characterisation. Now they were ready to go through the same procedure with the Mazurka.

Soon the dancers understood that in their performance of the character dances it is not so much the steps that matter, but the way these movements are executed. So afterwards, when we worked on the actual choreography with Delibes' music, the dancers were ready to portray these movements with great distinction in the right style. They genuinely enjoyed executing the choreography in this new light and that, in turn, showed in their performances. Instead of "dusty" or "moth-eaten", their delivery became fresh and sparkling, noticed by audience and critics.

Inventiveness or Authenticity?

In 1963 the Royal Opera House added to its repertoire a new production of Mussorgsky's opera *Khovanshchina*. I was asked to choreograph for the Opera Ballet the "Persian slaves' dance" in the 4th scene and, in the same act, a simple dance for the ladies' chorus (Russian serfs) while they were entertaining Prince Khovansky with their songs.

By that time of my career I was very much aware that when in the western world traditional classical operas, ballets or plays are renewed, they are produced and conveyed often in quite a different manner from their original productions. Sometimes they are modernised, shortened, placed in a different century from the one their creator intended, and often infused with some contemporary ideas, while trendy messages become emphasised. Sometimes costumes and scenery are changed and therefore, I believe, the inserted character dances should be composed and performed in a manner to fit this reformed style. In the case of this *Khovanshchina*, I learned that the director of the production wished to stick to its original style, except for cutting the length by leaving out a few scenes – a common practice with this opera in the majority of opera houses.

I was familiar with some older, rather beautiful Soviet and Hungarian productions so for me the simplest solution would have been to follow in the footsteps of these traditions. However, in order to avoid being trapped in a kind of quite fashionable attitude of "dogmatic traditionalism for the sake of authenticity", I wanted to have as much information and background as possible about this opera as a whole.

Before I started choreographing I had to find out how much authentic folk music Mussorgsky used in the dance scenes. So far as character dance was concerned, my aim was to follow a theory I believe strongly: the style of choreography should always reflect the accompanying musical composition style.

To my great surprise I learned that, according to musicologists, in the entire five acts Mussorgsky used not more than five authentic folk tunes. Unbelievably, he created the rest of this masterpiece without employing any traditional melodies. Due to his genius, as well as his love and knowledge of his native land's folklore, he dared to exploit to the full a creative artist's privilege, namely to invent in style. That is how he created this opera that is considered in the world of music to be the most Russian opera ever composed!

From the two melodies that Khovansky's serf girls sing and dance in the fourth scene, only the fast one is based on a folk song. For the singers I had to make the movements very easy, using the simplest of steps, arm and head movements that were typical of Russian folk dance, which could be accomplished by non-dancers.

The beautiful and haunting, rather sensual melodies of the "Persian slaves' dance" was also a creation of the composer's inventive fantasy. These had not much to do with any authentic 17th-century Persian folklore, but were based on music-images that were recognised in the 19th century as "oriental". Therefore I choreographed the dance with similar ideas in mind – the movements were sensual like the music. The images were strongly inspired by oriental drawings and paintings, in the same manner as the costume design. The producer, conductor and some members of the cast praised the musicality and the style of my choreography. There were similarly positive reactions from the daily press.

Dreams About Unity of Style

It has been always my conviction that character dance "inserts" in operas, plays and classical ballets should reflect the style of the whole production as well as its music. This idea was often put to the test whether I created dances for the stage, the small or large screen. Ironically, the most controversial challenge came from the direction I would have least expected. It was connected with the 1963 production of the Royal Ballet's *Swan Lake* at Covent Garden.

The producer was the world famous, Australian-born dancer, actor, choreographer and film producer Robert Helpmann. We had known each other since I was guest artist with the International Ballet of the Marquis de Cuevas, for which company Nijinska and he had produced an imaginative production of Tchaikovsky's *Sleeping Beauty*.

Frederick Ashton (the founding choreographer of the Royal Ballet, who had just become its artistic director), with Helpmann, was planning a new production of *Swan Lake* as they felt that the company's old one was a bit dated. While preparing this, Bobby (Helpmann) took his daily ballet lessons privately with me in my studio. He used to talk about the details of his ideas in connection with the planned production.

'Basically the ballet will not be modernised,' he explained, 'its story line and the time scale will be kept in the style of the old production.'. When he described how he wished to produce the third act and its character dances, he also asked me to choreograph them in this new production. I was delighted because I found his plans were exciting. At the same time I was surprised. 'What about Ashton's incomparable Neapolitan dance? This jewel of choreography is a "show-stopper" all over the world. Won't you keep it?'

'In this production I want all four dances created by one person – hence in the same choreographic manner – and produced as if the dancers were all under the evil spell of Rothbart. They're there to serve his sinister schemes'.

This was quite a thrilling concept! 'Choreographing the dances with this idea in mind challenges both performers and choreographer.' I said. 'The fact that not only Odile, but also the character dancers, are brought to the ball by Rothbart in order to help his schemes will change the meaning of these dances completely. The performers will have to express through their dancing not only the characterisation of their particular national identity, but they must show engaging court manners towards the Queen and Prince Siegfried, while showing servility and obedience towards their "employer" Rothbart as he gives them orders secretly throughout the scene with a conspiratorial smile.'

'Bang on! This is exactly what I am after.' he said enthusiastically. 'Just keep preparing in this way while I arrange for you to receive the contract, a rehearsal schedule and a meeting with Carl Toms, the designer.'

At last my dream was coming true. I was given a task to create and mould character dance "inserts" within a classical ballet in the style and meaning of the general production. It didn't worry me that I hadn't received my contract yet, I still urgently requested a schedule of my rehearsals.

First, I worked on the Hungarian dance, explaining to the dancers the whole plot. 'Each of you will appear as if by magic, conjured up by Rothbart, and freeze in a position for a few seconds, like robots. Only when he commands you to start dancing will you seem to become human beings. The usual vocabulary will be enriched with quite a few movement images that originate from folk dance. Some steps and *port de bras* that you and most of the profession mistakenly know as "Hungarian" will be changed in order to get the real style. In this production all the character dancers are creatures of Rothbart, so you'll have to make the audience aware of your evil nature with the use of some head movements, looks, eye focusing, gestures, etc.' Naturally the dancers liked the plot and all co-operated fully.

By now it was high time to start working on the other three dances, but there was no indication on the schedule for these rehearsals. I desperately wanted to give the artists ample time to get the choreography and the national style they represented under their skin as well as finding their own way for individual expression. The next time Bobby came to see my rehearsal, I asked him to urge the administration to act a bit faster.

'Oh dear,' he said in the most embarrassed manner, 'that is why I came to see you. I really don't quite know how to break the news I have just learned. Believe me, it's nobody's particular fault and no one meant to hurt or humiliate you. What's happened is due to chaotic organisation and bad communication amongst too many bosses. I understand that Rudi (Nureyev) offered to create a new arrangement of the Mazurka a long time before I came on the scene. Fred agreed and a contract was sent to him. I wasn't told about this until just now. Rehearsals for it will have to start next week.'

No denial, this was a bit of a blow to me, but I didn't want to show my disappointment to Bobby as I realised that perhaps his pride was hurt more than mine. Instead of licking my own wounds I tried to console him. 'As for myself,' I said, 'I don't mind too much about not doing the Mazurka. As for you, I am sure you will still be able to achieve your ideas for Act III. The main thing is that the scheduling of my rehearsals for the Neapolitan and Spanish dances should not be delayed any more.'

'But that's just it, Maria, I am so sorry. The latest decision is that you are doing only the Hungarian dance for this production.' (At that point I couldn't hide from him any more that I was shocked.) He continued to explain awkwardly, 'As the producer of the ballet, I had my rights to offer you the contract for all four dances. I had no idea that Fred already promised the Mazurka to Rudi. Neither was I informed that in his capacity as a director, he decided to keep the Spanish and his Neapolitan choreography from the previous (Sergeyev) production and the contracts concerning these dances were arranged before I made my plans and commissioned the character dances from you. I feel terrible about all this mess and for you being hurt so innocently, but all I can offer you now is the contract for the Hungarian dance, which you have already done. One may ask the question: what about the nice dream about uniting the Third Act and its character dances in meaning and style? I've ended up with the four character dances created by people with differing individual styles: yours in the Hungarian, Nureyev's in the Polish, Ashton's in the Neapolitan, and Ashton (after Ivanov and Gorsky) in the Spanish! In other words, the four dances will represent not less than five artists' individual styles, nestling within a ballet choreographed by six choreographers (Petipa, Ivanov, Gorsky, Goncharov, de Valois and Ashton). All together eight choreographer's personal styles in one ballet ... This must be a record number!'

'Think positive. At least the music is by ONE COMPOSER and in ONE STYLE!'

'Ha, ha, ha ... By the way, will you sue?'

'Under no circumstances would I do that, as my admiration for Ashton wouldn't let me do such a thing. Besides, that wouldn't be MY STYLE and who wants to deal with yet an additional style! Anyway, every wound heals with time, so will mine. In the meantime I'll try to consider the whole episode as a good lesson for the future.'

Indeed, I was soon given the chance to do all the character dances of *Swan Lake* with London Festival Ballet. I made use of what I learnt from the bitter lesson of this production that was well meant but – from Helpmann's and my point of view – quite disappointing.

Maria Fay in Budapest
Photos: courtesy of Maria Fay's family

Igor Moiseyev
Image by kind permission of the Igor Moiseyev Ballet

Maria teaching Gypsy Dance at Helen Wingrave's school 1958
The male dancer is Rudi Szegeti who helped Maria and her husband to escape across an icy river to freedom
Photos: Douglas Elston

Photos of Rudi Szegeti courtesy of his wife, Vivienne Hetzel

Rudi Szegeti and Wendy Hilton performed together in works choreographed by Maria during a summer season in 1958 at the Gaiety Theatre, Isle of Man, and for the Mondial Dance Company at the Festival Hall in London 1959

Photos: John Vickers/ArenaPAL (University of Bristol Theatre collection)

Maria and Rudi Szegeti dance demonstration 1957
Family album courtesy of Vivienne Hetzel

Family album. © *Vivienne Hetzel*

'Etude Caractère'
choreographed by
Maria Fay
The Royal Ballet School
Matinee at The Royal Opera
House June 1963
*All performance photos:
Fredericka Davis/Royal Ballet
School Special Collection*
By kind permission of
Sasha Davis

ROYAL OPERA HOUSE COVENT GARDEN

House Manager JOHN COLLINS

Royal Opera House Covent Garden Limited

General Administrator SIR DAVID WEBSTER

Assistant General Administrator JOHN TOOLEY

PRESENTS

THE ROYAL BALLET SCHOOL

Under the direct supervision of NINETTE DE VALOIS

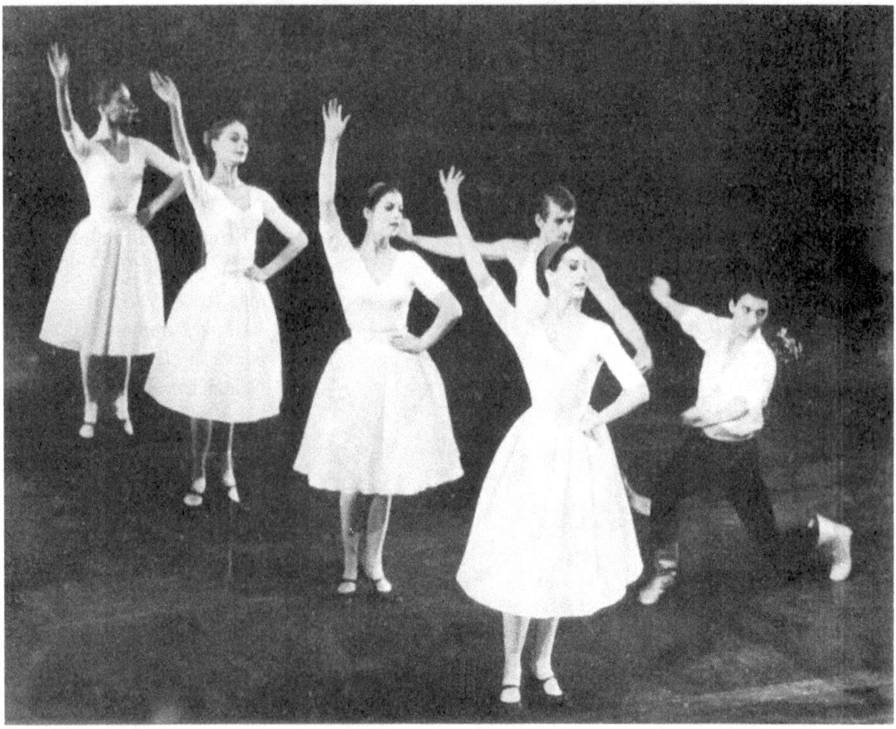

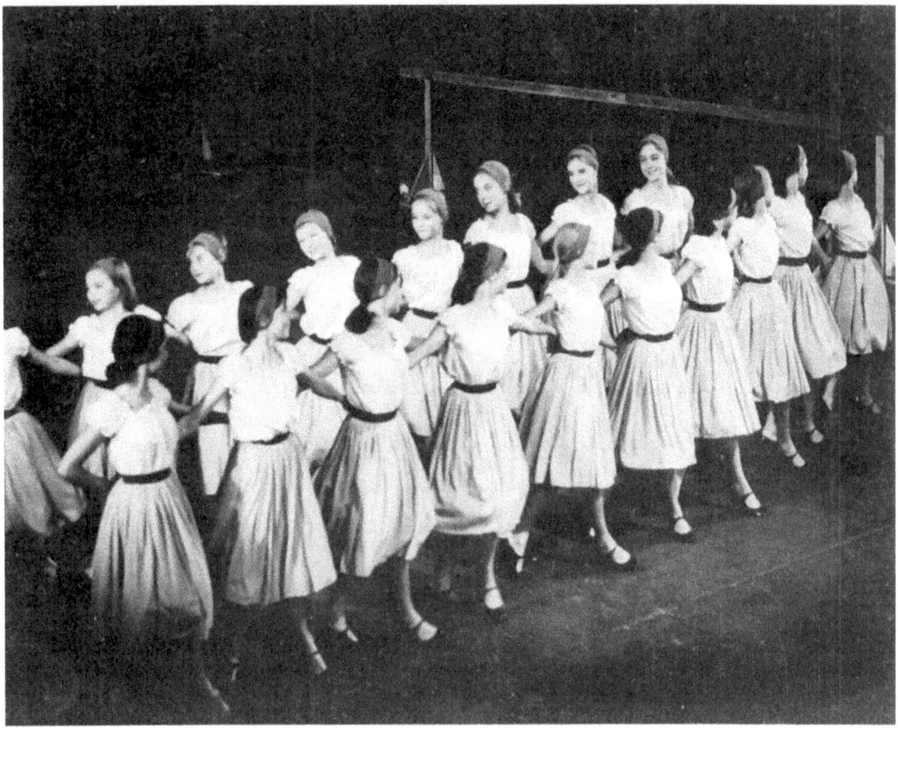

'Etude Caractère' curtain call
Photo: GBL Wilson/Royal Ballet School / ArenaPAL

Dancing Around the World
Students of the Nesta Brooking School

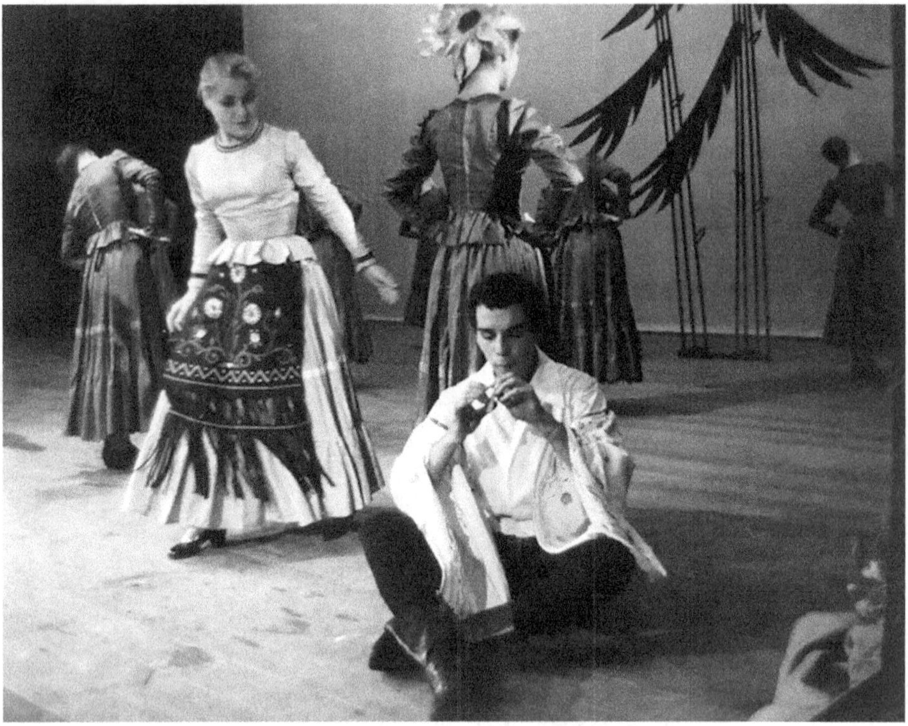

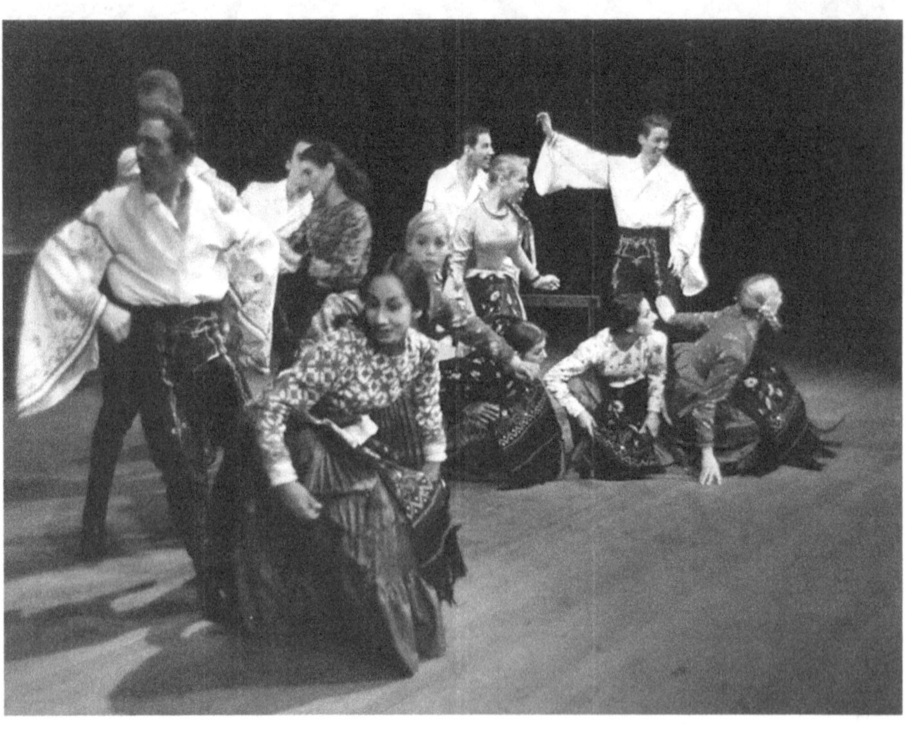

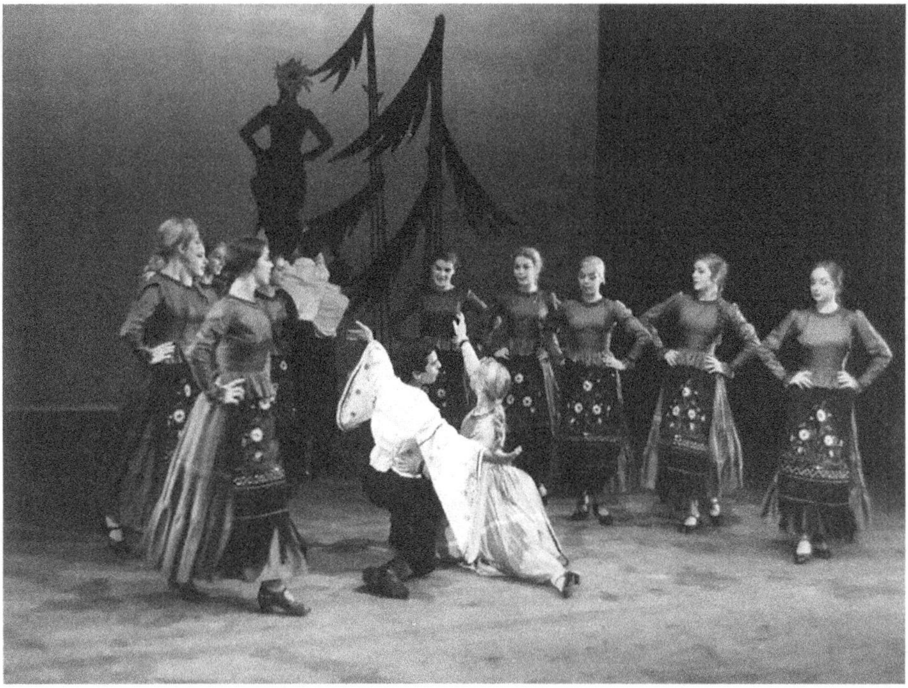

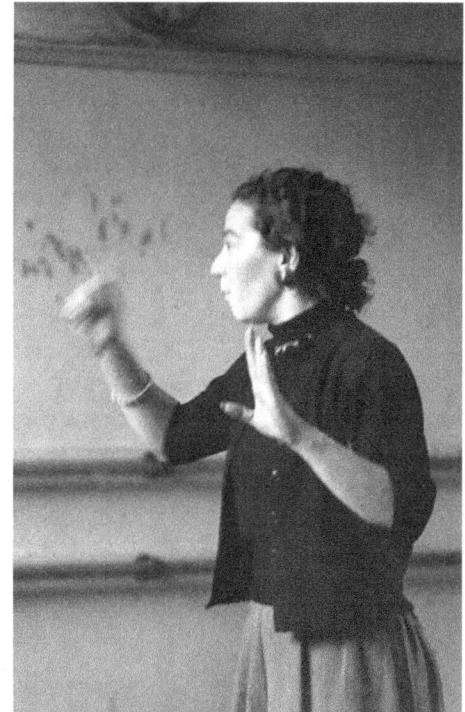

'De bloem van het geluk' (Lucky Flower) choreographed by Maria Fay in 1958/9 for Ballet der Lage Landen in Holland
Photos: Jan Dalman/ Dalman Productions
Courtesy of Elizabeth and Andreas Dalman

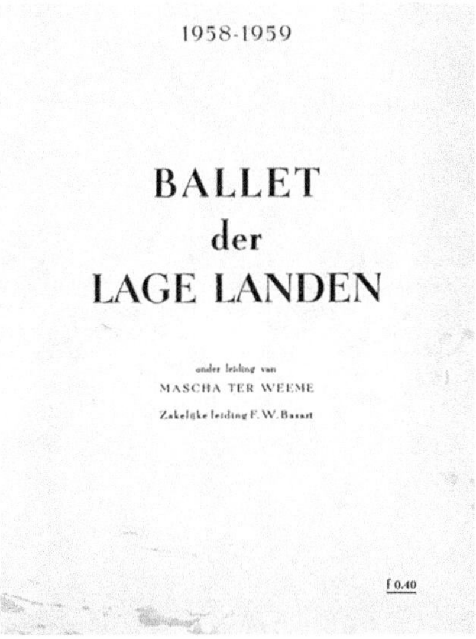

1958-1959

BALLET
der
LAGE LANDEN

onder leiding van
MASCHA TER WEEME
Zakelijke leiding F. W. Baart

f 0.40

Amsterdam Summer School
Photos: Jorge Fatauros

The Russian Dance choreographed by Maria Fay
John Field's production of Swan Lake The London Festival Ballet 1982
Photo: Anthony Crickmay / V&A Department of Theatre and Performance

Costume design by Carl Toms for the Russian Dance in Swan Lake
London Festival Ballet 1982
Photo: By kind permission of English National Ballet/V & A Department of Theatre and Performance

Fitting In

A short time after John Field took over the directorship of London Festival Ballet (now English National Ballet) he decided to replace the ensemble's production of *Swan Lake* – by Dame Beryl Grey – with a new one. He arranged to meet me and spoke about his plans.

'As far as the libretto is concerned I want to stick more or less to the original story except for the role and character of Rothbart. I plan for the First Act to be the usual informal outdoor birthday celebration for Prince Siegfried with his friends. The Prince should be portrayed as a bit of a daydreamer with a charming but indecisive character. One of his closest friends is the infamous Duke Rothbart who influences the Prince to lead an irresponsible and carefree lifestyle of drinking and flirting.

'The Queen Mother – who arrives in the midst of this informal party – makes no secret that she doesn't approve of this type of celebration. For his birthday she presents her son with a beautifully crafted crossbow, while she tells him that from now on he has to end his bachelor life, and she expects him to choose a wife at the ball that evening. To be forced into an unwanted marriage shocks Siegfried and he attempts to decline her wish, but she won't take "no" for an answer. The Queen suspects that the Prince's refusal is due to Rothbart's harmful influence, and in her anger she exiles the Duke from the court forever.

'The Prince seems to be so occupied with his own thoughts and his new gift that he doesn't even try to save his best friend from falling out of grace. The humiliated Rothbart swears vengeance. He knows that he has hypnotic power over the feeble, enervated and romantic daydreamer. As he leaves the Court, Rothbart turns towards Siegfried, and hypnotises him to go hunting swans at the nearby lake with his new weapon.'

I interrupted John enthusiastically. 'That would mean – if I am not mistaken – that in the rest of the ballet the realistic elements of the original synopsis are mixed with the fictitious imagination of the hypnotised prince. The reality of Siegfried's world are the scenes of the birthday celebration; the swan hunting; the ball and all the guests including the presence of the foreign princesses; the meeting with the strange but dazzling Odile; and the suicide of the Prince. However, the transformation of the birds into girls; the meeting of the mysterious, enchanted Odette and her jailer in the form of an evil owl; and Siegfried's vow to love and marry her; these are the result of a fantasy world created by hypnosis.'

'Just so! With this slight change in the libretto the majority of the original choreography is safe, but perhaps the whole story of the ballet will be more interesting and understandable for today's audience, or for that matter to a public of any time'.

'What are your plans for Act Three in general?

'The invited princesses will each represent a different country (Hungary, Italy, Russia, Spain and Poland) and will be introduced to the Queen and the Prince by their countries' ambassadors and their entourage (these are actually made up from the dancers who'll perform the character dances dressed in their national costumes.) Now, that's where I need your expertise. I would like you to create new choreography for not only the Russian dance – that was in the original score but has been used only in a very few productions we know of – but also for all the other national dances.'

'How do you wish to portray these people in your production? Do you see them as courtiers who represent the nobility of their own country? In this case the style and manner of my choreography – and of course the costumes – need to be rather formal with the emphasis on the elegance, refinement and courtly etiquette. Or perhaps they are professional performers in the service of their countries' royal family – in which case more folkloric elements and some spectacular bravura should be mixed with the court style.'

'I would go along with either of these suggestions so I leave that decision to you – as long as you tell Carl Toms in plenty of time so he can design appropriate costumes.'

I liked his ideas and found the whole concept interesting. I wished to become part of it, but, having once been the victim of a badly organised production plan with the Royal Ballet's *Swan Lake,* I felt that I'd better proceed this time with caution. I wanted to make sure that there was a viable production team which worked together right from the beginning, and would initiate me into its plans.

As it turned out I had no reason at all to be worried this time. All of us (designer, conductor, choreographers, stage manager, répétiteurs, rehearsal-pianists and dance-notators) made our plans together with John Field the director. Before the rehearsals started I received my contract. During the entire rehearsal period we frequently kept in contact with each other.

My first step was to get in touch with costume designer Carl Toms. We knew each other from when he designed the Helpmann *Swan Lake.* He showed me his new designs for the character dancers. I found them absolutely beautiful, and I was delighted with his choice of materials as they seemed to be light enough for dancing purposes. However, I was worried about the fact that he had designed hats for all the character dancers. Though they were perfectly designed in style, and correct if the occasion took place out-doors, for any indoor activity, court etiquette would never have allowed the participants to wear hats in front of the Queen and Crown Prince.

I was told that the simple reason for this was that in this company there were not enough female *corps de ballet* dancers to be split between "white acts" and the character dances in the Third Act. The only solution was for hats to be fixed permanently onto the character wigs that would cover the swan girls' hairdo. It was faster and more practical to put a wig with the hat already fixed on top of the dancers' swan-hairstyle: this would keep their hair underneath in a neat and tidy condition for the last scene at the lake. All they needed to do was just to put the swan's feather head-dress on their hair. Naturally, if the girls were to wear hats, their partners had to have them also.

These arguments were convincing and I had to go along with them in spite of my dislike. I understood that finding a better solution and a rational reason for solving this contradiction might come, perhaps, from how we would package and fit the character dances into the story line of the ballroom scene. After a lot of thought I came to the conclusion that the dancers should appear as professional entertainers giving an already rehearsed and planned performance for this special occasion on the Prince's birthday. Giving the character dances this background would explain the dancers' appearance (short-skirts, hats, boots, hair ribbons, etc.) at a ball given by royalty. It would also account for a freer and somewhat less formal dancing manner with elements of bravura. My concept was welcomed.

This solution came to me as soon as I started seriously studying the music composed for the Russian dance. Until that time I didn't know this beautiful composition. When I heard it, I just couldn't understand why this had been dismissed from the ballet. Tchaikovsky chose two contrasting folk tunes to create this real little musical gem. He composed a lyrical and poetical virtuoso solo for the violin based on the first folk song in which the orchestra joins gradually and they work up to a magnificent climax with the second melody.

When analysing the music of the Neapolitan dance I found that its construction was quite similar, but this time the trumpet was chosen as the solo instrument. In order to remain faithful to the style in which the composer created his music, I wanted to construct my choreographies on the same principles. As John Field had given me a free hand to cast ballerinas, principals and soloists for the leads, I had the means to equal the instrumentalists' sparkling virtuosity with the dancers' brilliance on stage.

At the first rehearsals I used my usual methods when given the task of choreographing character dancing. According to whichever nationality the dancers were representing, I gave them some brief background followed by corresponding barre and centre work. This way they quickly picked up the required style and in no time we could concentrate on the specific choreography itself.

The "performance" of these *Swan Lake* character dances opened with the Hungarian dance choreographed for five couples with one leading pair (ballerina Lucia Truglia with principal dancer Kenn Wells). This dance was always very well received by the audience, and, to everyone's satisfaction, the dancers' efforts were often rewarded by the audience shouting "bravo" even on those nights when the leads weren't danced by the first cast.

The Russian dance followed the Hungarian. Five girls in Russian folklore costumes, boots and hats were running playfully in a large circle suggesting they were five ponies pulling behind them a troika guided by the Princess, ballerina Andrea Hall dressed in a rich national costume, head-dress and pointe shoes. The five "ponies" were connected to the Princess by long coloured ribbons, which were attached at one end to the waist of each "pony" and the other ends were held in the driver's left hand, while her right arm moved as if gently encouraging her horses with a whip. Often just this "entrance" itself brought applause from the audience. (The idea of dancers imitating horses pulling a troika is a Russian folklore tradition.)

Then the driver halts and frees the girls from their harness, letting them turn speedily into their ribbons that fold around their waists tightly and then letting the ends go. In the music, the violin solo is a sophisticated and brilliant variation on a folk tune, so I choreographed for the ballerina a virtuoso variation incorporating original folk dance steps, hops, skips, turns *en pointe* with the corresponding folk dance *port de bras*. When the rest of the orchestra joins the violin, the "ponies" start to dance vivaciously with the Princess, doing the same authentic steps in their character boots as the ballerina does *en pointe*. Without fail this dance became a "show-stopper" at each performance.

Next on the programme was the Neapolitan dance. Again I just followed the pattern set by the composer. At the first slow part of the tarantella music, dominated by the trumpet player's lyrical and yearning variation accompanied by the tambourine, two couples and one principal male dancer (Matz Skoog) at upstage centre started a slow dance. The girls danced with tambourines while the boys (and leading dancer) had trumpets and, as they all moved in a lyrical and poetical manner, the boys mimed playing their instruments and serenading the girls. As the music became more embellished and lively, the male dancers laid their trumpets aside and joined the girls in a set of challenging fast-footed steps. Meanwhile the principal dancer joined in the "fun" with a virtuoso variation of dazzling, fast *petite allegro* and *grandes pirouettes* downstage centre in the tarantella style. To everybody's delight, this Neapolitan dance also became a "show stopper".

It is mainly the orchestration of the Spanish dance's music that gives the piece its magic and the flamenco-like style. The kind of Spanish character dance I learned as a young dancer was very theatrical as well as exciting. It was used in ballets performed in this manner by almost all the nations belonging to the Soviet Union as well as in other "iron curtain" countries. It was only after I came to live into the west that I had the opportunity to see the real thing. I not only watched with admiration flamenco dancers display their traditions, but whenever I had the chance I studied with some of the faithful disciples of flamenco "gurus".

As far as the style of the music allowed – similar to the other pieces I created for this production – I wanted to base my choreography on folkloric tradition. In this case I chose a custom where a female dances while showing off her colourful shawl. The fast and crisp rhythms tapped by the feet executed in a constantly held *demi-plié* had to be matched with the specific peacock-like posture of a Spanish dancer's sensually provocative manner.

The ballerina (Janette Mulligan) with two male soloists achieved an impeccable technique and style. I wanted the male dancers to behave in a "macho" manner and express rivalry towards each other, at the same time wanting to win the attention of both the girl and their audience. She behaved as if taking this for granted and pretended to hardly notice their efforts while dancing in a playful manner: enticing, but "hard to get" without becoming coy or vulgar.

As a finale of the character dance display came the Mazurka. I chose six couples to dance this piece, led by Caroline Humpston and Michael Pink. In this specific dance-style the most typical element is a kind of fast and elegant travelling – almost as if the dancers were skating – yet keeping the movements absolutely smooth. The steps, jumps and skips are not meant to attempt height but should be performed with the aim of covering distance, almost sliding over the floor. To have some contrast, this smoothness must be broken from time to time with various sharply-accented "break-steps" performed in various rhythms. This meant that, apart from teaching the dancers the style with the correct musical timing of the mazurka, I focused my choreography on creating often-changing floor patterns while covering distances on the stage. The music of Tchaikovsky's Mazurka is beautiful but, at the same time, it is the longest of the character dances in *Swan Lake*. The task: to execute the often, fast changing patterns, covering big distances whilst controlling the rapid movements with elegance during the length of the piece, demanded from the dancers perfect style and a lot of stamina. The appreciation of the audience was well earned.

During the "performance" of these character dances the Queen was seated at the side of the stage. I made sure that when each dance finished the dancers turned towards the Queen and made their first bows facing her and the surrounding courtiers, as well as the disguised Rothbart, in the style of the court etiquette. In turn the audience on stage applauded them. Only after that did the dancers face their "real" audience in the auditorium, bowing and receiving the ovation.

Character Dance Via Air Mail

∞∽∞

While I was teaching and choreographing character dance, many of my colleagues tried to convince me that it would be important to make written records of my entire character system. Though I agreed with them about the necessity, I didn't do much about it.

Quite a number of dances that I choreographed were already published by several dance institutions and dance teachers' organisations. In certain RAD syllabi there were not only the written notes of the choreographies, but also the corresponding barre and centre-exercises with the appropriate music which were given to those attending training courses. By then, certain choreographies of mine were recorded in Laban notation by some of my professional students. However, deep down, I didn't feel it was quite the right way to preserve my system.

By that time my work was taught all over the globe by a great number of teachers who learned it – or bits and pieces of it – directly from me or from the first generation of teachers who had studied with me. My character system had already been part of the regular curriculum at the RAD Teacher Training Course. Every year about a dozen students of this organisation received their teacher's diplomas and became ready to teach my system.

In addition to these young graduates there soon came others, but from a different source, as Dame Ninette de Valois had created a similar course. This was at the Royal Ballet School and was originally called a "workshop" for training young choreographers and teachers (this later became the RBS Teacher Training Course). She invited me to teach my character system on this course.

Apart from all these young teachers whom I had taught myself, there were a much greater number of teachers and examiners who – without studying my entire system – also taught some of the dances I had choreographed. They belonged to several teachers' organisations that invited me, or some of my disciples, to several of their refresher courses. We were asked to give lectures as well as to teach some of my dances which were suitable for different aged groups of children and students.

As a rule these organisations took it for granted that the invited lecturer will have prepared notes that can be handed over to all the participants after the lecture and sent out by post to absent members. I tried to "slip out" of this "note-writing duty" by claiming that – being a foreigner – my English wasn't up to the standard. (By the way, this wasn't just a shallow pretext, it was absolutely the truth.) However, several generous colleagues offered their help. I was treated like a spoilt child. 'You mustn't worry, just choreograph and teach the dances. The notes will be done.'

At the time of this offer I didn't quite realise myself that, with the best of intentions, these dear friends took out of my hands all control over the notes. It was a bit later when I became aware that these descriptions were written in a shorthand style, and that for some specific movements these scripts were using expressions in a general way. This meant that the wording from the style point of view was not describing the movements adequately. For example, "walking step", "*pas de bourrée*" or "country *pas de basque*" are mentioned frequently in the description without the slightest hint of the style in which these movements are supposed to be executed. These steps exist in almost every nation's folk dance traditions but, from the style point of view, they are entirely differently performed in the various countries. These descriptions could easily mislead those people who might learn – and then re-teach them – only from these notes.

Many teachers and examiners started to complain that this pollution was happening, and warned me that to rescue the work from misinterpretation it should be written down both in English and as dance-notation.

The Benesh Institute decided that it wanted to have in its library a record of my entire character system. For this reason they arranged that one of their members – Melvina Burra – should study with me. The Institute supported her in having regular private lessons with me, in order to learn and record my character system. To chose Melvina for this work proved an excellent decision. This young lady seemed to be not only very interested in the subject matter but also extremely intelligent. She was blessed with exceptionally sensitive style-awareness and musicality – two crucial qualities for character dancing. She was diligent enough to cope with taking in and processing such a vast amount of material in a comparatively short time. She picked up even the smallest particulars concerning the given style.

We established a working routine. Before she started to study a specific style, I always gave a short historical background of the nation or ethnic minority in question and a description of some of their national customs. Only after this introduction did I start to teach her the corresponding barre exercises, and in the centre she learnt the steps and their variations that were used in the dances. After our class she made detailed notes.

At the following lesson, instead of me teaching her any new material, I asked her to reproduce everything she had learned on the previous occasion, but I didn't allow her to reproduce anything from her memory. She had to read first all the movements from her Benesh notation script and then to execute them accordingly. I was adamant that she should demonstrate clearly, in the correct rhythm and even the smallest detail of every movement – including how the torso, head, arms and hands are related to each other. I called her attention to how important it was to notate even the direction in which the eyes should focus. We worked like this for several months and were happy with the results, as we had achieved – at least for those who were trained to read Benesh notation – the build up of my system, and its preservation, with precision.

The Benesh Institute's aim to have a record of my character work was obviously so that in the future it could be read – and perhaps re-taught – by anyone familiar with this notation. However, there was something about this "preservation" which made me uncomfortable. Instead of being flattered that these professionals found my work so worthwhile that they wished to protect it from being forgotten, misunderstood or misinterpreted, there was still some resistance from me. Why?

It occurred to me that Melvina's notes would be studied by several professionals who hadn't studied my system either with myself, Melvina, or any of the first generation of followers. I had no doubt that people trained in this notation would be able to reproduce the movements containing my system with precision when reading these notes (after all, that must have been the goal for making and safekeeping these records), but it worried me that, by only reading the notes without ever studying physically my work with experts, would they be able to achieve the style, liveliness and theatricality that is the essence of the system? Without these qualities one would end up just re-teaching a large collection of lifeless barre exercises and steps.

Looking back now, I suppose my hesitation in this matter was understandable. Fifty years ago both the Benesh notation and my character system were just "promising toddlers", so to speak. Both needed time to be tested in practice, corrected and expanded to how we know them today. At that time a first class choreologist could record quite precisely any movement, as Joan Benesh and Melvina Burra showed me when we first worked together on my character system. However, I felt that as far as specific style and quality of the movements were concerned, something was lacking in the actual script. This made me somewhat uneasy, as the essence of character dancing on the professional stage is the style and quality of the movements. The rhythms and the technicality of the steps are only the pegs on which this can be hung.

Nothing upsets me more than seeing any type of dance system of value being taught dogmatically, as an accumulation of "fossilised" movements – no matter how correct they are technically. Alas, it can happen too often in several of the traditional dance teaching systems. I felt, however, that a lot of people in the profession didn't see this problem my way and some of them perhaps thought me too fussy or even pompous. I remember quite a few occasions that made me realise that in this matter some of my colleagues – even those who were sincere friends – had very different views from mine.

One day I received a letter from a South African teacher who was an RAD examiner and also in charge of a highly considered ballet school in Johannesburg. She explained that so far she had been unable to work with me in person, but she had studied my character work and dances from the notes that were published in the latest ISTD syllabi and she liked them very much. She had a couple of talented 13-14 year-old students whom she'd like to dance some nice character solos – which were not in any syllabi – at her end-of-the-year school performance. She commissioned from me a mazurka and a Gypsy dance and I was to send the notes to her by post. She offered me quite tempting fees.

I couldn't believe my eyes! To commission choreographies "via airmail" – just as one would order by phone a take-away meal – seemed to me simply a ridiculous situation. I was convinced that this must be a unique case and the teacher a particularly odd person.

Next day, at one of my regular classes for teachers and professional dancers, I told them the story about this "eccentric" teacher – without telling them her name – thinking that they would find it as absurd as I did. With the exception of the dancers, to my great surprise most of the teachers who were in class didn't find the situation funny at all. Some senior teachers explained that this case wasn't an "odd" one: 'In that part of the world,' I was told, 'it is a well-established practice that overseas teachers regularly buy, via airmail from teachers whom they consider experts, various choreographies suitable for student displays. This "trading" is quite usual and the price of a solo choreography, especially if two are ordered at the same time, is normally much less than you were offered by this teacher. You should realise that to be commissioned and, what's more, to be offered a higher fee from the usual price proves that she treats you not only as a reliable expert, but she considers you also as a "celebrity" teacher'.

Oh dear, I didn't realise that my attitude towards "sending choreography by mail" might have been taken as an insult. I suddenly saw myself as a bull in a china shop. I never brought up this subject again. However, I answered the colleague in South Africa in a polite letter saying that I was unable to fulfil this commission. Nevertheless, my refusal and my opinion generally about this whole matter must have become known in the profession, as I never ever had any more such commissions, and I was quite glad of it.

Teaching and choreographing character dance was a very important issue in my life but it was only one line of my professional interest. My involvement with teaching and coaching classical and contemporary dancers held for me just as much importance, challenge and fascination.

Apart from being very busy working with classical dancers in my own ballet studio, as time went by, more and more ballet companies and vocational schools, in Britain and abroad, invited me as a guest teacher and coach. I was seriously involved with the systematic training and coaching of professional dancers and also with their rehabilitation and prevention of injury. I felt that the procedure of becoming part of dancers' technical and artistic progress was a great responsibility, and I owed to those dancers who trusted me and expected my help as much of my time and energy as I could muster.

To fulfil the demands of both my character and classical ballet teaching and coaching jobs became quite trying, and sometimes impossible, especially when my guest teaching was abroad. The obvious answer to this dilemma was that it was time to gradually "delegate and share" my duties in both subjects. I had to work out a viable plan.

For my character dance teaching it was a bit harder to find the right solution, but by this time I already had a few very talented followers of my character work who were prepared, ready and willing to teach my system. So, in some of the key-positions, where my work had become part of the regular curriculum, I suggested to the directors that, while I am out of the country, some of my most reliable and talented graduate teachers could continue to teach my character system. Then, if this solution proved to be successful in the short term and if both management and teacher agreed, it could easily become a permanent situation. The directors understood my problem and I had their support for this plan.

Ursula Morton and Valerie Adams welcomed Valerie Sunderland (originally a student of the school) both at the Royal Ballet School and at its Teacher Training Course in my place. Soon the directors, teacher and pupils found this arrangement so satisfactory that Valerie remained the regular character teacher at the latter establishment.

For the next few years I still kept teaching my system at the RAD Teacher Training Course and was looking for a suitable candidate to take over from me permanently. At that time one of the excellent graduating students was Virginia Parkinson.

I knew her previously from Banff (Canada) where, during a summer course, she studied classical ballet with me. Later, when she moved to London and enrolled at the RAD Teacher Training Course, whenever her timetable allowed, she participated in the professional ballet classes at my private studio. Hence, Virginia became familiar with my outlook on our art form in general. To understand and convey correctly the technical material and the essence of my character system seemed natural to her. Keith Lester, the director of the course, totally agreed with me that she was the best possible candidate for this job. Indeed, she proved to be one of my best disciples. She taught my system on this course and elsewhere for the next few decades.

Both Valerie and Virginia kept in touch with me regularly and, of course, I was always delighted to see their excellent work. We kept helping each other whenever it was necessary. When Valerie was pregnant, Virginia stood in for her at the Royal Ballet School, and by the time Virginia got in the same boat, Valerie was ready to continue there. Much later, when I didn't need go abroad so often, I myself took over for a couple of years these classes when Valerie became so busy (as a major examiner for the RAD) that she was unable to do the work.

I also hoped that some of the great number of young teachers who studied with me, Valerie or Virginia, and graduated from the courses, would convey correctly my system when fulfilling their teaching posts all over the world. Indeed, there are quite a few who do excellent work. On the other hand, there were many who would have liked to teach character dance the way they learnt it from us, but in some schools the directors hindered them from doing so. Unfortunately, in these cases the quantity of the finished "product" mattered more than the quality. They were often put under pressure to teach the children in character classes only dances taken from various syllabi of the different dance teaching organisations. The timetable didn't allow them the necessary time to teach systematically, including the corresponding barre exercises and centre *études*.

These were frustrating experiences and the outcome was disappointing but, as everything depends on the attitude and aims of the various directors of dance schools, teachers must follow their director's ideas. We can hope that, with time, more and more people in the profession will realise that, if one wishes to avoid injuries and at the same time to achieve good artistic results in character dance teaching, one has to convey the subject in a systematic way. This approach needs a bit more time and patience at the beginning, but, in the long run, it actually saves time and one gets more valuable results.

Both the good and bad experiences made it obvious that recording my system would be important, if it could be done in such a way that it wouldn't become fossilised and that everybody in the profession could read and understand it. I came to the conclusion that the only solution would be to make a videotape or DVD of it, where one could see clearly in detail the construction of the build up, technique, quality of the movements, style and performance combined with the correct and stylish musical accompaniment.

But it isn't enough to have the knowledge, some well-trained dancers, suitable studios and a willing film crew to achieve this aim. What one needs most importantly is the help of one or more generous sponsors. Needless to say, sadly, they are not queuing up in front of my studio, so I just live in hope that perhaps one day this might turn into reality: "Where there is life, there is hope!"

Through the "Dark Ages" to the "Renaissance"

My teaching experiences in the profession taught me that one has to have an open mind and be constantly alert to what the progress of the art-form demands of the dancers. As the art of dance continuously evolves, one has to mould and adapt the teaching systems for teachers to follow accordingly. This is especially necessary when one is dealing with professional dancers and vocational students. For the same reason, artists who create a teaching system – whatever the subject – must be broadminded and flexible enough to scrutinise and, if necessary, revise their creation from time to time.

Perhaps there are some "rules and principles" that have been correct and helpful to dancers at the time when a movement-system was created, but with the greatly changing demands on dancers some of them might become out-dated or superfluous and even harmful to the interpreters' physical wellbeing.

During the last four decades a second and third generation of teachers have taught my character system continuously and successfully. Despite my not teaching it regularly, I kept in touch with these teachers and scrutinised my system frequently. I had reason to be fairly confident about the basis on which the whole system was built – as this was the main factor that has earned the most appreciation from performers, teachers and accomplished leaders of the western dance-world in this time. However, it would be big-headed and short-sighted of me to believe that there is nothing in the system that needed changing. A work that one started in the fifties, and in a completely different background, must require some re-thinking sixty years later given circumstances that are constantly progressing.

In the last decades the most important symptoms of these changes in the profession were due to the fact that technical demands on dancers became more stressful than ever. Working together with orthopaedic specialists, physiotherapists, osteopaths and masseurs, most of the accomplished classical ballet teachers who worked in professional companies and vocational schools changed some of the old rules. At first only a few dared to initiate these changes and experiment with some new ways to protect the over-worked dancers' vulnerable muscles. Many of these alterations were concerned with warming-up before the daily barre exercise, the order of the exercises in the barre-work itself, the controlled breathing technique, and the "cooling off" after the lesson.

Gradually more and more teachers followed the "idea", but the exercises and the order in which they were taught, were, and still are, individual. I welcomed these ideas in my classical teaching. Since my character system and the build up of a class were modelled on the rules of the classical ballet method, it seemed logical to follow suit and make similar changes in this system. The more so, because I found that as the art of dance expanded with all kinds of new styles (jazz, tap, contemporary, musical theatre, etc.), the timetables of most vocational schools became busier and busier every year. As a result character practice sometimes had to be the first lesson after the students' daily academic studies or on Saturday mornings. Therefore I created a special warm-up routine to be taught before the barre exercises, in order to make sure that in these situations young dancers should not develop stiff, heavy and unattractive muscles, and become prone to muscle fatigue leading to injuries. I found that this warm-up routine helped in injury prevention, particularly for the more adult or amateur students, and that it is better to place the *plié* exercises after the *battements tendus*. Also, I decided that the order of the positions in which the *pliés* are executed should also be changed. As the 2nd position is the less demanding on dancers' muscles and leg joints, I thought it safer to make them practise starting with the 2nd and then continuing with the 1st, 5th and 4th positions. For junior students (or amateurs) I suggested leaving out the *grand plié* in the 4th position. I found this most important in order to avoid the overstraining of the hip and knee joints, the Achilles tendons, as well as the thigh and calf muscles, before the young dancer's body is ready for that extreme position (alas, this happens so often).

For the same reason I became adamant that, in character studies, one should be even more careful than in the classical classes that during the barre exercise dancers should not bear the weight of the body for too long on the "inside" leg, especially where some *fondus* are involved. Apart from the danger of building overly bulky muscles, it also "nails down" the dancers, making them earthbound instead of mobile. I believe that one of the secrets of a good dance technique – whatever the style – is the ability to change the weight of the body, rapidly and "seamlessly", while executing all differing movements; "melting" one movement into another with a continuous flow. The barre exercise must be the dancer's preparation for the centre work (dancing on the stage) from every artistic point of view concerning technique, style and quality of movement.

One of my main concerns was to make the system more concise, because the ever-changing choreographic demands on dancers made their life even more overloaded. In order to condense the system, I decided that first I needed to polish and emphasis those elements that enhance the dancers' theatricality, style awareness and technique. Having done this, I could then eliminate those elements that proved to consume much more time than their usage justified, and some of those which might have caused confusion in differentiating the various national styles from each other. (This kind of problem often occurs when teaching some movements in the Polish Mazurka and the Hungarian Court styles that are somewhat similar.) What determines the style – in the case of these steps – is the way in which these movements are executed, like emphasising the slightly differing rhythms, and the *port de bras* with typical shoulder and head movements. Hence one should teach and focus on only one version of a step that makes it typical of the specific style which the dancers are studying or representing on the stage, and do away with the confusing ones.

I also added more technically demanding exercises, especially for the male dancers, according to the students' progress, as long as the virtuosity – like pirouettes, diagonal turns and high jumps – could be kept within the specific style they were studying. All these changes and additions proved to be positive moves in the right direction, and were welcomed by those teachers then in charge of teaching my system to the new generation of dancers and teachers. However, one couldn't help noticing that there seemed to be a contradiction, in that the profession's interest in character dancing declined around the last decade of the last century. Why did this happen?

With philosophical resignation, I thought that we were simply witnessing a typical "three-day wonder" situation that occurs from time to time in every performing art, and one just has to face this declining interest as a "morning after effect"... But deep down I had the "gut-feeling" that this situation might not be final. It dawned on me that "when in doubt turn to history" and viewing the last decades through dance history in general might give a more logical and less pessimistic answer.

No performing art form can survive without its performing artists and an audience. The new types of creation (including the *l'art pour l'art* choreographies) draw a public that appreciates and understands the freely chosen idioms, as well as the original ideas that contemporary artists are conveying in their works. The larger the public, the more performances are required, and that, in turn, demands more dancers who are trained to be versatile enough to interpret the numerous styles and techniques that all these various creations demand. To fulfil these tasks, new types of specialised vocational schools were set up.

The list of these schools is endless. Naturally, the already established vocational and amateur ballet schools – which are amongst the profession's sources to supply the future generation of dancers, choreographers and teachers – had to expand and re-organise their teaching programmes. They had to accommodate in their timetables new subjects like Pilates, Yoga, various "body-conditioning" and "stamina-building" lessons, as well as contemporary, jazz and tap lessons, in often-overloaded schedules.

As the contemporary creations almost never used national or character dance elements, it is understandable that less and less time was allocated for character lessons in schools.

As mentioned before, for many teachers it became almost impossible to teach my character system faithfully, as the essence of the method was that the studies had to be spread out over many years, with each style being studied in blocks with the corresponding barre and centre exercises. Of course, to make these ideas successful is time-consuming and the school directors couldn't give enough time for the character studies. Many teachers were under pressure to compromise and just teach this subject in a commonly used way: giving at each class a sort of short "general character barre" for warm-up purposes, followed by some dances of the repertoire or arranged folk dances from the several syllabi that were on offer. There were quite a few teachers who hadn't even been given the time to teach at each lesson this "general character barre", and had to restrict themselves just to teaching various dances.

Although at times it seemed as if teaching character dance with my principle ideas had become an "unaffordable luxury" for most, there were still quite a few amongst my colleagues who managed to stick to my principles and "carried the torch". That was just as well because after a few decades, in the nineties, the tide started to turn.

The more our art form has progressed, the more obvious it has become that a versatile physical training – one that prepares dancers' bodies to execute all kinds of movements belonging to different movement-regimes and styles – wasn't quite enough. The importance of serious style studies – a kind of training which will equip students to be able to pick up quickly the styles from differing movement-techniques and those according to the personal style of the choreographer – became evident. Dancers, whose "bodies, ears, eyes and brains" were trained through my character system to differentiate the stylistic differences of various nationalities, found that when faced with any kind of movement-techniques and choreographers' personal styles they almost mechanically and instinctively noticed even the slightest differences. This way – to the delight of the choreographers, dancers and répétiteurs – they quickly picked up the required style.

Sadly, there were only a very few professionals, amongst those who were in charge of preparing the new generation of dancers for their stage career, who saw the importance of students' and trainee teachers' detailed and refined character studies. However, Valerie Adams, the then director of the Royal Ballet School Teachers' Course and the Professional Teachers' Course never faltered. During her long directorship, she made sure that there should be always time enough on the course's timetable for experts to teach Spanish Dancing. She also insisted on having my character system taught and examined. Valerie Sutherland kept teaching my system for a long time, and I examined the trainee students myself, until she decided to give her entire energy and time to her job as an examiner at the Royal Academy of Dancing.

This coincided with a period when – due to my husband's life-threatening illness – I stopped guest teaching abroad and stayed in London permanently. So, when Valerie Adams approached me to teach on this course regularly again, I was happy to do so and retired from it only when she did so herself.

The other institution that still saw the importance of character dancing was the RAD For decades, at their Teachers' Course, Virginia Parkinson taught my system with great results until the RAD's reorganisation, when the whole course was dispersed. So, the "Dark Ages" weren't quite over ...

A real "Renaissance" started soon after Gailene Stock took over the directorship of the Royal Ballet School.

We knew one another from way back when she was a young student newly arrived from Australia. She had been offered a place in the Australian Ballet but was too young to sign a contract (in Australian law), so she was given a generous scholarship to study for a year in London: mornings at the RBS, and afternoons with a teacher of her choice. She chose to attend the professional ballet classes I taught at my private studio, where she worked tirelessly on her classical technique.

Her talent, musicality and sensitivity for quality were obvious from the beginning, but what was most remarkable for her tender age was how seriously she took her studies and how "over-critical" she was about her own work. Also, she reacted with maturity to corrections given not only by me, but also from some of the professional dancers who attended the same classes. She seemed to analyse her mistakes and consequently make the corrections. (Many years later I found out that, of her own accord, she had even written down all her classical classes and kept them for future reference.) At that time I was teaching my character system regularly at the RBS on certain mornings, and she also studied this subject with me.

Through her personal experiences she realised that studying seriously classical ballet simultaneously with my system of character dancing does not injure or over-develop young dancers' muscle structure and, at the same time, awakens students' receptivity towards the various national and personal choreographic styles. Probably these facts spurred Gailene Stock to "re-introduce" my system in the school. After all, these were the same reasons that made her famous predecessor, Dame Ninette de Valois, establish my system in both the RBS and its Craftsman (Teacher Training) Course.

Not long after she took over the directorship of the RBS, she contacted me because she wished to place the senior students' character studies in the hands of a teacher who had studied my system. There was no such problem at the Junior School, as by that time the subject was taught by Tania Fairbairn. A gifted dancer with stage experience, she is an excellent teacher and has an unusually broad view of character dance, as she worked with several experts from abroad as well as with Virginia Parkinson, Valerie Sunderland and myself.

Unfortunately, owing to the health problems of both my husband and myself, I could not undertake to teach the subject regularly any more, so I suggested Valerie Sunderland for this job and agreed to give some master classes occasionally. Thus Valerie decided to take the "baton", as it were, again and, with her renowned precision and demanding high standards, continued to do so for two years. Sadly, we were forced to look for another suitable candidate to take over from her, when she was obliged to give up because of a knee operation as well as the growing demand for her services as an examiner with the RAD. After careful consideration Valerie came up with the perfect answer. She suggested Amanda Maxwell, a former RBS graduate and dancer, to take over.

I knew Amanda from the time when she graduated from the RBS. Her stage personality was quite obvious, even in the classroom. For the following years of her professional career, I coached her regularly in the various classical roles she was given to dance. Curiously, the opportunity of working with me on character dancing (something that happened with the majority of soloists that I regularly coached in classical work) just never occurred. However, as a young student in the RBS, she had studied my system with Valerie Sunderland. I lost contact with her when she retired from the stage to become a wife and mother.

I met her many years later when I was invited, as usual, to examine the trainee students of the RBS Craftsman Course. To my great surprise Amanda was one of the examinees. I was told that she had enrolled to get her teaching diploma from the Professional Dancer Teachers' Course. As it happened, this highly intensive one-year course's densely-loaded timetable could not include character dance studies. Against all odds, Amanda was determined this time not to miss out and asked permission from the course director to join Valerie Sunderland's character classes at the Craftsman class that was being examined by me. Her excellence in the subject and her beautifully stylish execution of the movements in some of the études was no surprise to me at all.

When Valerie Sunderland suggested that Amanda would be a suitable candidate to take over her post at the Upper School, I was more than happy to support the idea. As we – and especially Amanda – all knew, her studies in the subject were short and incomplete. I promised to broaden her knowledge. In the following years her excellent and inspired work proved over and over again that she was an "ideal teacher" and the best choice for the job.

Both Amanda and Tania Fairbairn felt the need to know more details about each other's work, goals and achievements. In this way the junior students would understand how their early studies connected to the later ones in the senior school, and they would be able to continue to build on the solid base already received. With Gailene Stock's help we organised a kind of regular "workshop" at the Upper School, where Tania, Amanda and I worked together revising, collating and checking notes of the vast material available, and I also contacted Virginia Parkinson who willingly agreed to join us.

Her contribution was most useful. Her recollections of the way I had been teaching the trainee teachers were most helpful in the effort to keep my system from calcifying when teaching it again to promising young professional dancers. Besides having precise notes from her original studies, she was able to remind me of some of the important details of how I explained the quality and style of various movements. She also remembered, and connected, the ways I analysed some intricate movements and split them into small details in order to be able to re-teach them correctly and make it all alive again.

Later, we welcomed to our workshop the former dancer and choreologist Fiona Cater, whose work was warmly suggested to Miss Stock and I by Elisabeth Cunliffe, director of The Institute of Choreology. It was felt that it was about time that the old script of my system, recorded about fifty years ago by Melvina Burra and then preserved in the Institute's library, should now be updated. Though Melvina did a brilliant job, Benesh notation has improved beyond recognition since then, and become recognised in the professional world of our art form. Needless to say, I had also changed and altered quite a lot of my system during these five decades. Fiona's aim and interest was to make a faithful score of my system as was taught at the RBS by Amanda and Tania. This precise record is now placed – together with its relevant music – in the Institute's library as well as amongst the files of the RBS for future reference. This will enable all those many dancers and teachers, who in the last half century have studied and re-taught my system, to refresh and update.

Fiona has done this work with diligence, intelligence, precision and enthusiasm. She showed a special keenness in learning and being able to dance and demonstrate all the movements herself. All of us in the workshop felt it was a pleasure to have her input and were pleased to see that the more knowledge she gained from the system, the more she wanted to learn about it. Her valuable contribution was essential in bringing this book to its conclusion.

Part II

Description of
Barre Exercises and Centre Practice Steps
for
Character Dance Classes

*with Maria Fay's Notes
on the style and quality of movements*

Contents

Class in Hungarian Court Style	99
Class in Polish Style	107
Class in Hungarian Gypsy Style	117
Class in Georgian Style	125
Class in Russian Style	133
Class in Romanian Style	143
Class in Hungarian Peasant Style	151

The classes outlined in Part II of this book were given some years ago, and form the foundation of Character Dance classes that were taught at the Royal Ballet School by **Amanda Maxwell** Dip. RBS TCPD ARAD and **Tania Fairbairn** Dip.RBS (TTC), ARAD AISTD (CB), B.Phil (Hons).

The exercises were recorded with Benesh notation by **Fiona Cater** DPMN ARAD Dip. PDTD. Samples of this notation including descriptions and analysis by Maria Fay are available for reference in the Royal Ballet School Special Collections. It is intended that the Benesh notation will also be available online for viewing and to download by going to the following internet page: www.powerop.co.uk/mariafay/

The exercises listed here are numbered and cross-referenced with the Benesh notation: a number and a title in **bold** indicates an item of choreology. Related items eg **1)** *Révérence* (ladies) and *Révérence* (men) are grouped together or identified as eg **17a) Slow lejtő, 17b) Quick lejtő**. In other instances variations of movements are labelled eg **9)** *Adage* **movements A and B**. In this, our presentation has been constrained by the original material.

Maria Fay has always stressed that her system is not 'set in stone' but should evolve to suit individual classes and their teachers: what is shown here is not suggested as a 'rigid syllabus'. In reproducing just the accompanying text from parts of the original notation, the editors have incorporated amendments, as advised by Amanda Maxwell, in order to bring the account more up to date. We hope that, in spite of some discrepancies, the relationship between the revised text and the choreology will be easy to follow, and that this historical record will offer an interesting insight into Maria Fay's Approach to Character Dance.

HUNGARIAN COURT STYLE

As its title indicates, noble elegance and a refined manner are more emphasised in the study of this style than would be usual in the original national dances. Though some steps and rhythms have a connection with Hungarian peasant dancing, the majority of such movements – being naturally rural, down to earth and unaffected – are unsuited to dancing in the sophisticated dresses of the aristocracy, gentry and upper-middle classes at their balls. So several dancing masters of different nationalities made up the movements incorporated in the 'Hungarian Court' style in the 18th, 19th and early 20th centuries, and taught and choreographed them accordingly. It was a showy and well-loved style, gradually becoming popular, and danced in most European courts and in many classical ballets.

HUNGARIAN COURT STYLE CLASS

1) *Révérence* (ladies)

Révérence (men)

This 'Révérence' is used at the beginning and end of each class to acknowledge the musician and the audience. With the first one, the dancers face the pianist (conductor), with the second they face the teacher (audience).

2) Preparation for all barre exercises

This movement is used before each group of barre exercises. The beginning of the arm movement is executed with an impulse and is quite dynamic. As the arm gradually circles upwards/forwards, the movement slows gradually (rubato) and becomes more controlled at the moment when the hand is placed with fingers on the hip. At the same time the upward movement of the head is accented with a proud expression.

+ (Analysis of *port de bras*)

BARRE EXERCISES

All barre exercises are related to some of the steps performed in the centre practice.

An explanation for the unusual order of *battement tendu* and *plié* barre exercises shown here, and in some of the notated classes in other styles, is given on page 89 of Part I.

3) *Battement tendu*

As the style of these leg and foot movements demands a brittle, staccato performance from both the supporting and the working leg, it is important that – after having done just a few in succession – one inserts a 'break' movement, placing the weight on the alternative leg. Then repeat the *enchaînement* reversed.

4) *Pliés* (in 2nd position also performed in 1ˢᵗ, 4ᵗʰ and 5ᵗʰ)

+ (Alternative use of top)

The rising up from the *grand plié* – in contrast to the downward movement – is a slow and controlled movement that changes into a sharp accented one when the outside leg moves into the next position.

5) Break A and B

Various 'break' movements used between phrases are typical in this style. In order to avoid injury or cramped muscles, it is advisable to include them often when practising strenuous movements in a series at the barre and later also in the centre.

6) *Battement tendu jeté*

It is a common mistake that the dancer leans more in a diagonal forward direction instead of bending the torso exactly to the side over the working leg. As this exercise is rather demanding on the supporting leg, it is wise to interrupt it from time to time with the 'break' movement.

7) *Rond de jambe à terre*

The *en dehors* movement of the leg is executed in an evenly controlled slow and smooth way (legato) and with a majestic quality; while the *en dedans* movement is fast and abrupt likewise in reverse.

8a) *Port de bras* (ladies)

These movements are continuous, adage-like and danced with a flow. A common fault might occur in the deep back bend if the dancer breaks the neckline by dropping the head too low. The same applies in the forward bend. Men also perform this exercise but with much less back bend.

8b) Rocking (ladies)

In this movement the toes of both feet must be kept together. The torso bends gently sideways with the arm in the 5ᵗʰ position and the palm of the hand facing forward. The whole movement has a lyrical quality and reminds one of corn in the

HUNGARIAN COURT STYLE

field blown by a gentle wind. The male dancer performs the step as well but not with this *port de bras*. He might place one or both hands behind the nape of the neck.

9) *Adage* movements A and B

In the *adage* movements A and B, dancers have to avoid a strained performance. In order to achieve absolute controlled fluency and highly-elevated leg movements, the muscles of the abdomen and the back must be involved and combined with the correct breathing technique. This way the *port de bras* will become the natural result of the leg and torso movements.

10) Preparation for *Promenade*

During all barre exercises, the hold on the barre must be very light with hardly any weight placed on it. This way the dancers will achieve 'independence' from it. As a result, when later dancing in the centre, fluency and travelling will become natural. This principle must be especially emphasised in this exercise.

11) *Grand battement* A, B and C

The abdominal and back muscles have to be much involved when practising these exercises, as well as correct breathing technique. This will enable the dancers to perform the movements later at great speed.

12) *Cabriole*

At the beginning, it is best to practise *cabrioles* at a slow speed while facing and holding lightly onto the barre. This way the dancers have support, when practising how to land from their jump and how to control the noise that the wooden heels of their shoes or boots might make on landing.

CENTRE PRACTICE

It is characteristic of this style to place strong emphasis at the end of some specific movements or at the end of a succession of movements. If this is disregarded – even if the movements are otherwise correct – the dancing will not represent the style and, what is more, might become boring and meaningless.

13) Slow walks

In these steps, the weight of the body is placed immediately on the front leg while the other leg is slowly 'dragged' towards the supporting one as if 'almost late, but still in time' to close the movement with an accent.

14) *Promenade* A and B

Here the most important feature is that the emphasis is placed on the last movement. It should start with the two slow walks (dragged) while the *port de bras* is carried out majestically with a smooth legato style, moving the arms fluidly around *en dehors* (as a windmill). The flow of the leg movements is suddenly interrupted with the high reaching *développé ballotté* and the skip on the supporting *relevé,* whilst the arms continue their smooth circling movement. A common fault in performance is to start this motif with the *ballotté* and then follow with the slow walks.

15) Rocking (ladies)

16) *Renversé*

Renversé sauté

Whether it is performed as a slow *adage* or executed with a *sauté* (men's version), the climax of this movement is always when the moving leg reaches the *croisée derrière* position in *fondu*. The hand of the moving arm touches the nape of the neck with emphasis.

17a) Slow lejtő

There is an impulse on the up beat of this step that fades away gradually during the rest of the movement, as the weight of the body is placed onto the forward stepping leg. As the torso leans slightly backwards, the back leg is slowly dragged towards the 1st position.

17b) Quick lejtő

Whilst in the slow lejtő the battement is done at a 90-degree height, in the quick version the height is at a maximum of 45 degrees and the head and torso movements are also smaller accordingly.

17c) Quick lejtő *en arrière*

It is advisable to practise this while travelling towards *effacé en arrière,* as the step does look lighter and more theatrical in this position and direction.

18) *Retiré*

This step is easily confused with its Russian counterpart, the virvyiovoshka, as on the surface it is very similar, but in reality they have very different characters and are differently emphasised. The latter is kept all the time on *demi-plié demi-relevé* keeping the torso *en face,* while the Hungarian version is all the time accented upwards and danced on a fully-stretched less deep supporting knee and *demi-retiré*. It can be accompanied with the Hungarian *port de bras* using *petits épaulements.*

(The notation includes a **'Sideways dotting'** exercise at this point with the following comment:

'While the supporting leg is energetically "stamping" and the other leg sharply "stabbing", the dancer is travelling towards the supporting leg's side while the arm is moving elegantly in a very fluid vertical circle *en dedans* whilst the torso is bent sideways away from the supporting leg.'

A **'dotting'** exercise is, however, more commonly included in Russian Style classes.)

19) *Cabrioles* **A and B**

In both versions (A and B) the steps must be executed forwards and backwards travelling fast, noiselessly and covering space.

20) Bell Step, **kis harang** also known as **harangozó**

The Hungarian name for this step means 'little bell', as it is lilting and tilting to-and-fro like a pendulum. Its specific rhythm should not be changed.

Pirouettes

21a) *Attitude pirouette* (men)

21b) *En dedans pirouette*

It is important in this style – as in all other character styles – that the *demi-plié* in the preparation of all kinds of *pirouettes* should be very powerful and fast, but hardly noticeable. All the *pirouettes* have to be executed with their character *port de bras* as in the notation. The men have to take great care of the position of the hands and fingers that are just slightly rounded, not tightened into a fist.

Diagonal turns

22) *Chassé coupé en tournant*

23) *Posé* **turns**

In both the *chassé en tournant* and the *posé* turns, the arms are not used in a balletic way. The ladies hold them either both on the hips, or one on the hip and the other in 5th position, or with fingers to the nape of the neck. The men may use the same as the ladies or both arms in 2nd position.

Turns on the spot

24a) *Attitude relevé* **turn** (ladies)

In this turn, in order to stay on the spot, it is not enough to control the supporting leg; the working leg has to touch the floor always precisely in 5th position *en arrière*. The *port de bras* helps the speed of the turn if it is done completely parallel with the working leg.

24b) *Attitude sauté* **turn** (men)

This turn, by its nature, cannot be performed at the same fast speed as the previous one.

POLISH STYLE

In the classical repertoire the Polish style is also often used. The dances of the Polish nobility, unlike in the case of Hungarian dancing, do not differ greatly from their peasant origin. Only the polonaise, often danced in the ballroom, has no folkloric roots. Both the krakoviak and the mazurka were as popular at Court balls as they were in folk dances, though the tempi of the latter are usually faster than their ballroom counterparts. The polonaise and the krakoviak are technically much simpler than the mazurka, so it is advisable to teach those to the junior students, leaving the mazurka studies for the graduates. All these dances, in more technical and demanding forms, found their place in classical ballets and operas.

POLISH STYLE CLASS

1) Position of the hands when on the hips

It is important, right from the beginning of these studies, that the dancers become familiar with the correct posture and arm position when the hands are on the hip. It is a common mistake that the dancer lets the elbows drop backwards. The correct posture of this basic character position is that, while the shoulders are pulled and locked down, the wrist and lower arm are held in an unbroken line and the elbows are pulled slightly forward.

2) *Port de bras* analysed A and B

When the arm moves in front, some dancers drop it with a little swinging movement (almost 'drawing' a horizontal figure of eight). This seemingly tiny misinterpretation causes a number of stylistic faults: the straight line of the arm gets broken by the wrist and the fingers get separated and somewhat rigid. As this *port de bras* is used later when performing the various break steps, and the many variants of the mazurka steps in the centre, it is important to get them absolutely right, especially at fast speed.

Make sure also that the head movement and the breathing are co-ordinated with the arm movements. From the point of view of style, it is important that although the leg, head and arm movements are smoothly co-ordinated, the accent with the head movement and afterwards the turn of the hand is performed with emphasis, but still in an elegant classical manner.

3) *Révérence* (ladies)

Révérence (men)

As in the Hungarian class, the *révérence* is done to acknowledge the pianist (conductor) and the teacher (audience).

BARRE EXERCISES

4) Preparations for all barre exercises

5) *Battement tendu* A and B

If the character class is the first of the morning, it would be prudent to start the class with *battement tendu* exercises and to practise the *plié* as the second exercise group. It is recommended to first practise the leg movements alone, and then to add the *port de bras,* as the co-ordination of these is rather difficult.

6) *Pliés* (in 2nd position also performed in 1st, 4th and 5th)

Although the start of each *plié* is emphasised with the head and the arm movements, the action is absolutely controlled by the leg muscles, as it is in the classical practice.

7) *Battement tendu jeté*

This exercise is preparation for one of the best known krakoviak steps. The leaning of the torso away from the working leg must not result in arching the back or a strained neck. The diaphragm and the muscles of the back have to control this position. The supporting leg should make a sound, but this stamping action must be controlled in order to avoid possible injury to the sensitive metatarsal. It is advisable not to repeat this movement too many times without interrupting it with some restful movements (such as preparation for *pas marché*).

8) Preparation for *pas marché*

By using the *demi-plié* for advancing forwards and backwards, this step must be kept on one level. The dancers should imagine that whilst dancing they have to carry an object placed on the top of their head.

Breaks

9a) Half break analysed

The half breaks – as all break steps – are performed not only to break up a series of steps, but are often danced in the centre in their own right. It is useful to practise them at the barre combining them with other movements.

9b) Full break

At the beginning of studies, accompany the leg movement with the Polish *port de bras* using the same arm as the moving leg. Later use the opposite arm to the leg. One can practise them alternately.

10) *Rond de jambe à terre*

This exercise demands a deep *fondu* on the supporting leg. The *port de bras* moves smoothly and elegantly. While the torso is leaning away from the moving leg, the tummy and back muscles must control the unbroken diagonal line. At a later stage it is nice to hold a *balance* on the moving *relevé*.

11) *Retiré*

This is often used as a linking movement rather than as a step on its own. It can be performed with or without a stamp.

12) *Battement fondu tombé*

The rhythm and emphasis of the *fondu* exercise is the preparation for the mazurka. Common faults are that the dancer is just a fraction late with the preparation on the up beat and/or dropping heavily, and with a noise, into the *tombé*.

13) Heel clicks

This exercise is to prepare the small *cabriole* and the holubetz step for the centre practice. After repeating it several times, it is wise to break it up before repeating it again.

POLISH STYLE

14a) *Grand battement*

14b) *Grand battement* to the side

Although both versions of this movement are, like the *fondu* exercise, for preparing the mazurka step, they should be practised at first at a slow speed. Only when the dancers can perform with precision and ease should they practise them at the speed of a court mazurka.

15) Holubetz

There must be hardly any weight placed onto the hands on the barre, so the dancer can easily proceed in travelling to the side. At the moment of the jump, the torso has to be tilted over the jumping leg. At the same time the head is turned and lifted over the jumping leg. After a little while, one should leave only one hand on the barre and with the other arm do the typical holubetz *port de bras* and head movement as when danced in the centre

CENTRE PRACTICE

16a) Half break

16b) Full break A and B

The various versions of the break step can now be performed and combined with the differing versions of the 'Polish' arm movements (opposite arm, same arm, and two arms). This step is used in almost all Polish dances.

Polonaise

This dance was well known and danced in every European court and middle-class ballroom in the 18th, 19th & early 20th centuries. Its popularity was due to the fact that it was easy to master and it was suitable to dance in elaborate costumes and head-dresses and in various formations (in couples, holding hands or dancing individually). This was the best way to be seen by every guest in the room – and at the same time for the dancers to be able to see the important people standing around. After all, this was the reason for being there.

POLISH STYLE

The polonaise has to be performed with grace and a majestic hold of the torso. It consists of only one basic motif that can be performed travelling forward and backwards and creating various floor-patterns. Due to these characteristics it is widely used on the professional stage.

A common fault when dancing it is to hold arms at the height of a 2nd position. Originally the ladies held their arms with grace just above their crinolines and held their skirts lightly with their fingers. When dancing with their partners, gentlemen must hold their partner's hand at that height.

17) Polonaise sample basic step

Krakoviak

The krakoviak (like the mazurka) was, and still is, a folk dance that was specially favoured by children for its fast speed and simple rhythms. They found that dancing it was good fun. For the same reasons it gradually became popular also in high society ballrooms where the krakoviak was danced in couples.

18) Heel clicks

The turned-in 2nd position *demi-plié* must be done without making a sound, in contrast to the *relevés* in the 1st position where the clicking of the heels should be heard clearly. Later, in centre work, this step can be performed not only on the spot but also with each movement sliding slightly backwards, creating diamond-shaped floor patterns.

19) *Galops*

Whether dancing this step in pairs or individually, the torso must be bent exactly sideways and the arms must not 'dangle'. To avoid this, the control must come by locking the shoulders firmly downwards. It is a common fault that dancers bend forwards and sideways, instead of only to the side.

20) Dotting step

This step has already been prepared at the barre in the *Battement tendu jeté* exercise. It can be performed individually or in couples; danced on the spot or; travelling forwards with each 'dotting'; by stamping with the supporting leg or without making a sound.

21) Pivot turns

At the beginning of the studies do this step with quarter turns, than with half turns and finally with whole turns. Both genders may do them with one arm in 5th position or just hands on hips.

22) Krakoviak *pirouettes*

Most of the time the *en dedans* version is used without the 'turned out' *passé*. It is important that it has a quick preparation from a deep *demi-plié* without the balletic arm position. The number of turns in the *pirouette* is not important, what counts is the style and speed with which it is executed.

Mazurka

23) Pas marché A, B and C

Versions A, B & C play an important role in Polish dancing in both folk and court mazurka. All versions of this step travel as much as possible by placing and keeping the torso forwards and keeping all the steps on the same level. The *demi-plié* must be used for elongating the step forwards instead of emphasising its depth. (If this rule is neglected the dancing will look like a Tyrolian ländler or a waltz). The torso and the head are held completely motionless. It should be practised forwards but also travelling backwards, in circles, in straight lines and in couples.

24) Balancé and *chassé relevé arabesque* A and B

These steps have the same stylistic features as prescribed in the *pas marché*. (The *balancé* travels far to the side and is kept on one level while the torso is controlled.) In the *arabesque* the torso is continuously moving forwards.

24C) Turning *balancé*

This turning step is also kept on the same level and the step on the *plié* has a tendency to travel far (contrary to the style of a waltz).

24D) *Balancé* with *pirouettes*

This combination of movements is often performed in some of the stage versions of the mazurka. Depending on the choreographer, it can be executed with *en dehors* or *en dedans pirouettes* but the best loved and most stylistic version is to do it with *en dedans arabesque derrière pirouettes*.

25a) Mazurka A *(Pas Mazur)*

The accents of this step are on the up beat (using the little jump as a move forwards) and then on the first beat of the bar, doing a *tombé* forwards while carrying the weight of the body continuously forwards. In the *pas mazur* – as in the *pas marché* and the *balancé* – the movements are far travelling and are kept on one level. They can be performed accompanied by *port de bras* of one or both arms.

25b) Mazurka B (turning)

One has to aim for performing half a turn on each mazurka step. The first half turn is *en dedans*, the second turn is *en dehors*. In both the A & B versions, the top is always completely square and kept *en face*.

25c) Mazurka C

In this version the torso is kept above the back leg, the arms are in a low diagonal with the palms turned upwards and the torso gently turning to *petits épaulements*.

26a) Holubetz (analysed)

The magic and the style of this step depend on the sophisticated co-ordination of the arm, head, and leg movements. The swinging of the arms inward starts with a strong emphasis, underlined by the head movement that comes up with the landing from the jump.

26b) Holubetz and *balancé*

This is an ideal form for the male dancers to practise the holubetz as a high jump using the *balancé* to alternate sides.

26c) Holubetz with *grand développé sauté* (male dancers)

This is a 'bravura' step for the male dancer. The energetic *port de bras* and the position of the fingers must not get out of control.

27) Small *cabriole* turns

Both genders can execute these turns individually in a series as a 'turning on the spot' version of the *cabriole*. With one step and jump, a whole turn is executed. With time the dancer should achieve a rather speedy performance. It can be danced also by couples standing side-to-side to each other, having one arm around the partner's waist while facing in opposite directions with their bodies. They perform small *cabrioles* to the side and, by doing a small step forward after each *cabriole,* the couple keeps turning around fast. This version can be danced by two men with highly extended *grandes cabrioles*. In this latter version, the speed of the movement is slower.

HUNGARIAN GYPSY STYLE

Gypsies live in almost every country of Europe, Asia, the Americas, Australia and Africa. There are differing theories about their origin; some ethnographers believing that their roots are in India. However, it is agreed that they were a nomadic tribe travelling from the East towards the West. From time to time, a fragment of the tribe settled for a while as ethnic minorities in the different countries, while the others went on travelling until another part of the tribe settled temporarily somewhere else.

Wherever they made their 'temporary' home, they kept some of their own culture (language, music, dancing), traditional occupations (weaving, fortune-telling, iron-forging, entertaining with their music), and lived according to their own ethical morals and traditional rules. Wherever they settled, they picked up some of the language and music of their host-country and freely 'mixed and matched' these influences.

Evidently their dance culture went through the same procedure. One can find some of the same elements – typical Gypsy dancing; the way they dress; their jingling jewellery; the free hairstyle and in some places the tambourines they dance with– in every country. At the same time, due to the 'mixing and matching', their dancing and its technique are different in each country where they presently live.

However, in some cases the differences are marked, which proves that the Gypsies do not only evolve a specific style on their own and completely independently, but also keep it as a tradition without mixing it with foreign influence. The most outstanding example of this is the famous Flamenco style, with its castanets, costumes, music, singing, clapping and guitar playing, that was evolved by the Gypsies living in Spain. Indeed, this has not much in common with the Indian

Gypsy style (again something very special) or with the unique Romanian Gypsies' dancing traditions. All of these styles are again completely different from the dance style of the Gypsies who live in Hungary.

When watching Hungarian Gypsies dancing for the first time, it might give the impression of a lazy, uncontrolled and careless way of moving. In reality however, it demands a technique from the dancers through which they give the impression that they are just improvising on the spur of the moment and being totally carefree.

They dance often with a 'couldn't-care-less' expression and then, suddenly, they alter the mood expressing the opposite. There are often tempi changes too. In this rhapsodically changing style, many of the leg and arm movements are initiated outwards from the centre of the body, with a controlled impulse as if they would have been 'sent' into position and not 'put' there. However, the movements coming from the centre of the body start from an impulse (and not from a 'contraction' contrary to the Martha Graham-created contemporary style).

If this technique is achieved it excites the dancers as well as the viewers and musicians. This kind of atmosphere may lead to some spontaneous improvisation on both sides and, with time, can become an enriching addition to the tradition.

The men perform the same movements as the girls, as in the flamenco style, but always with a less soft (more 'macho') manner. Sometimes, they like to clasp their hands behind, on their lower back. Also, they like to dance while clapping improvised rhythms and tapping on their legs, arms, and chests.

The male dancers – just as in flamenco dancing – never touch their female dancing partners, although their dancing relates strongly to the women.

HUNGARIAN GYPSY STYLE CLASS

BARRE EXERCISES

1a) Standing position analysed

1b) Position of hands when on hips

1c) Finger click

1d) Shudder (shake) analysed

Before any of the barre exercises are taught, it is advisable to practise the technique of finger clicks and shuddering (shaking) of the top of the torso (analysed in the notation script). As the dancers become familiar with the Gypsy vocabulary at the barre and in the centre, one should add these gradually to the *enchaînements* in the barre work as well as in the centre. Add to these 'special preparing studies' the 'standing' position (analysed in the notation score), as this is also very different from the way it is in balletic and other styles.

2) *Révérence*

This is a motif that should be taught only after a few weeks of study.

3) Arm preparation for all barre exercises.

The impulse given to this movement is simultaneous with the finger-clicking and it gradually dies away as the lower arm is semi-circling. A common mistake is that, during this movement, the dancer lets the elbow of the working arm leave the torso.

4) *Pliés* (in 2nd position also performed in 1st, 4th and 5th)

Each *plié* starts with a small impulse. A frequent mistake is that, instead of circling the pelvis vertically with a straight controlled back, the dancer does this circle horizontally.

5) Battement tendu

In this style, the actual *battement tendu*s happen as a result of the starting impulse from the centre of the torso. The closing of the *tendus* are rather 'fading withdrawals' of the leg into the starting position. The head and arm movements are the natural result of the impulse and the 'withdrawal'.

6a) Rond de jambe à terre en dehors

6b) Rond de jambe à terre en dedans

This exercise is performed with the same technique as the *tendus*, but the starting impulse has to become even stronger in order to achieve the impression that the *rond* itself is just 'happening', 'fading', and 'withdrawing' into the position.

7) Petits battements

A common mistake is that the dancers make too big a movement with the lower leg. This slows down the speed and makes it look clumsy.

8) Rond de jambe en l'air

The arm and the flicking hand movements should look as if they are encouraging the leg movements. This becomes even more emphasised with the accompanying *top work*.

9) Battement fondu

Here again, the turning-in and turning-out of the movement just 'happens' with the starting impulse from the centre of the torso and is 'helped' with the slaps on the upper leg. One can take a balance after the last movement in the *à la seconde* position, taking the hand off the barre and executing claps or finger clicks with both hands in the chosen rhythms.

10a) Grand rond de jambe jeté 5/8

After the *coupé*, the front leg is raised with an impulse given from the torso and 'sent' into its high *rond* with the slap on the upper leg.

10b) *Pirouette en attitude en dehors derrière* **or** *en dedans en avant*

These are used often as a break after performing a series of *rond de jambe jeté*. The arms are in the 5th position and the top of the torso is bending over the lifted leg.

11)   Grand battement développé soutenu 7/8

+ (with higher extension)

The whole movement is initiated from the centre of the body. The torso must not make a backwards or forwards bend, but it 'arrives' naturally with a 'fall' backwards/forwards and the head and arm movements are almost late. The arm is not 'put' to its position, it just 'happens' to get there with a relaxed quality. At a later stage, when performing these movements with a high extension, it is important to emphasise these impulses even more than when they are performed with lower extensions.

12)   Grand battement balancé

After the beginning stages, this movement can be performed so that, after having done the exercise a few times, the dancer takes a balance on *relevé* and, at the same time, turns the top into *épaulement* with a finger click.

CENTRE PRACTICE

13)   Promenade

It is a common error that the dancer swings the arms without controlling their height (the lower arms and finger-clicks should be at waist level and the upper arms below shoulder level). In spite of the head turning slightly towards the left and right, the eyes focus on a point in front.

14) Transfer of the weight

This step has to be executed with the same technique as used in the *plié* exercise at the barre. The movement is initiated from the pelvis movements. In the accompanying *port de bras,* both elbows have to be kept close to the torso.

HUNGARIAN GYPSY STYLE

15) *Grand rond de jambe jeté*

This step at the centre is performed with the same technique and quality as practised already in the barre exercise. The *coupés en avant/en arrière* and the slaps on the thigh are the initiating impulses.

16) *Pirouette en attitude derrière en dehors*

The entire *pirouette,* as well as the circulating parallel arms, is all initiated from the starting *coupé* in front. The torso is slightly bent backwards over the lifted leg.

17) *Pirouette en attitude devant en dedans*

The rules are the same in this *pirouette* as in the *en dehors derrière* version. The arms are held in a loose 5th position over the *attitude* leg, with the upper body lying towards the lifted leg and the head slightly drooped forwards. (Both *attitude* turns are used, almost as a break step after a series of *grand rond de jambes* is completed.)

18) Pivot turns on the spot

The first step across in the deep *demi-plié* is emphasized with the *renversé*-like top, while the arms are in 2nd position and the elbows drop at the same time as the fingers are clicking. The elbows lift again during the on-the-spot turn which is executed with the second step. Spotting takes place to the front, but the entire body should always face to the side.

19a) Parallel *pas de chat*

When performing this step, the deeper the dancer keeps the *demi-plié* while leaning forward over the legs, and the faster the movements are while travelling sideways, the better.

19b) Arm taps

The taps on the arms must have a very sharp and broken quality, while the torso and head movement, initiated by the transfer of the weight, is performed with a contrasting flow and smooth quality.

19c) *Rond de jambe en l'air*

As practised at the barre, this 'irregular' *rond de jambe* is performed with vitality.

20) Heel *pas de Basque*

To execute this step in style, one has to execute it in deep *demi-plié* and with a forwards-bent torso.

21) *Petits battements*

This step was already practised at the barre. It is used in the centre as if propelling or encouraging oneself to move.

22) Gypsy *bourrée*

This is performed with a sense of exuberance and should be executed fast and travel far.

23) *Grande sissonne*

The grande sissonne should have a feeling of 'flying through the air'.

24) Rhythm Step (There is no notation for this step.)

There are several ways of utilising travelling steps with differing rhythms and syncopations. Amongst all the steps performed in this style, this movement perhaps is the one that must give the impression of most uncontrollable temperament, yet this is the one that demands the most disciplined co-ordination.

Diagonal Turns

25) Pivot turn

The style of this turn is exactly the same as in the 'turn on spot' version. At a more advanced level, the dancer (both genders) may do a *pirouette,* finishing on the knee at the end of the diagonal.

26) *Petit Pas de Basque en tournant*

This turn must be performed at a fast speed keeping a deep *demi-plié* all times while the arms are in 2nd position and the elbows drop and lift in the same rhythm as the fingers click. The arms and torso work with the same technique that was used in the 'pivot turns'.

GEORGIAN STYLE

This beautiful style is danced in the Caucasus and it is strongly influenced by Persian, Turkish and Arabian dances. It proved to be a worthwhile study for professional students (especially for female dancers) even if the overall ballet repertoire doesn't include Georgian dances as such. In contrast to oriental styles that require many years of special study (double-jointed and extremely pliable bodies are needed to perform Chinese, Indian, or Javanese dances), for the classical ballet-trained female dancer it is possible to acquire the unique technique of the Georgian style in a shorter time. Mastering this style is very beneficial, if choosing carefully from the rich movement vocabulary. Furthermore the special stance that this technique demands will enrich the dancer's back control – which will become a great asset to the general technical standard of any dancer. Practising this style regularly with its barre exercises will definitely not cause any injury or develop heavy or unsightly muscles.

The stance is the secret of the female dancers' feminine and almost 'magical' gliding. The specific movements of the shoulders, upper-arms, elbows, wrists and fingers are due to control from the back and the placement of their body weight. The mastery of this back-control actually can be extremely useful in all the romantic ballets when portraying swans, butterflies, fairies, Wilis, and so on ...

To capture the athletic bravura of exciting male dancing is more complicated for dancers whose ambition is to become a member of a classical company. To achieve and practise some movements of the Georgian male-dancers' 'dazzling' technique might certainly lead to over-developed thigh muscles or end up causing injuries for knee, ankle and toe joints. Just to mention a few examples: a *tour en l'air* finishing on both knees, fast *ballonnés* jumped on the toe-knuckles, breathtaking *chaînés* in a circle on the knees and *pirouettes* on the knees whilst the men hold drums in their arms and swords in their mouth.

However, there are several beautiful traditional dances, for male dancers only, where the technique doesn't demand this type of athletic bravura. Their specific and incredibly speedy footwork; the way they perform high jumps, or when they are accompanying the ladies like shadows expressing a chivalrous and protective behaviour towards the opposite sex, is all based on the back control that is useful for every kind of male dancer. To dance the fascinating dance-rhythms and sophisticated phrasing is also educational.

In the Georgian dances, the dancing style of the two sexes is so contrasting that it would be unwise to teach men and women at the same time in one class, especially in the early stage of the studies.

GEORGIAN STYLE CLASS

Right from the beginning of these studies, one has to concentrate, not only on the precision of the movements of the arm, but on the co-ordination between the work of the torso, head, arms, shoulders, fingers, legs and feet. When these are more or less harmonised, one could add the technique of working with a scarf. (Its corner must be held between the first and second finger.) In order to use it successfully, without ending up with the scarf wrapped around the arm as often happens, the scarf should be of silk or some very light material that has a similar flow.

When teaching barre exercises in the Georgian style, it is advisable to follow this method:

- Teach first only the leg movement (so this becomes automatic).
- Practise the *port de bras* separately from the leg movements and with the corresponding music.
- Combine the arm with the legwork.
- Add the head – and if necessary – the shoulder movements.

At first glance, this procedure may seem time-consuming, but, in the long run, it saves time and gets the required result.

1a) Analysis of *Port de bras*

The first two vertical circles of the arm are executed with a feminine and smooth quality, while in the third one the flicking of the hand is sharp. That quality changes again into a soft and lyrical movement when the arm reaches downwards across and on the side of the leaning torso.

1b) Analysis of *Port de bras* with scarf

The hand-flicks have to be executed with purposeful sharp movements of the wrist in such a way that the scarf reaches a vertical position with each flick of the wrist.

2a) Preparation for all barre exercises

This is performed before each barre exercise.

2b) Bow

Executed at the end of all exercises at the end of the last phrase. It is performed especially when dancing in the centre with the opposite sex, but also when dancing with the same gender.. It is an expression of traditional politeness, but executing it often during the class is also a very sensible way of stretching and resting the dancer's back, neck and shoulder muscles after such concentrated use.

BARRE EXERCISES

It is important that the exercises are executed in long skirts.

3) *Battement Tendu*

The torso (leaning away from the working leg) must be controlled from the muscles of the back and the tummy so that it never becomes arched. The quality of the movement is smooth and lyrical.

4) *Pliés*

In the *demi-plié,* the first two circles of the arm are executed with a feminine, smooth quality, while in the third one the flicking of the hand is sharp. The quality changes again into a soft and lyrical movement when the arm reaches downwards across the leaning torso.

As this *enchaînement* of variant *pliés* is all done in the 6th position, it is advisable to repeat the combination only three times on one side (or even just twice, if the dancers are warmed-up already) and then, with a half turn, to continue on the other side.

5a) *Rond de jambe à terre*

5b) *Rond par terre*

The leg is moving continuously in a smooth way during the whole phrase, while the liquid flow of the hand and arm movement is sharply cut when closing the legs in the 6th position. The unusual phrasing must be strongly defined with the sharpness of the hand and head movements at the end of the phrase.

6) Toe tapping

The accenting with the head happens together with the sharp heel-tap. The toe-tapping is light, though definite.

7) *Grand battement ballotté* **(3/8)**

The bouncing *demi-plié* on the supporting leg is as even as a metronome beat. While the arm is moving smoothly, the hand is flicking with sharp accents, simultaneously with the knee bounces.

8) *Développé soutenu*

Both the arm and the leg movements start with an impulse on the first beat that gradually calms down until the sharp accented movement on the 7th beat. The leg is not lifted higher than a maximum of 60 degrees.

CENTRE PRACTICE

All the barre exercises, including the accompanying *port de bras*, are performed in the centre in combination with the specific gliding, walking, dotting and other travelling forwards or sideways motifs. Depending on the *port de bras* in question, the dancer can now perform them with each doing either the same or a different *port de bras*.

9) Gliding

In the Georgian style the gliding walk is most typically performed by the ladies. Whether the steps are slow or fast, the top is lifted with the chest pulling the weight forward. Whichever arm movements accompany the gliding, the shoulders are pulled down from the shoulder blades and the head is held erect. The steps are executed keeping the upper legs fairly close. Common mistakes are to tilt the neckline with a lifted chin and/or arching the back.

10) *Développé* walks

The lifting of the knee in the *développé* must be prominent and just high enough for the skirt to swing a bit upwards so that, in the next movement, when the dancer steps forward onto her heel, the edge of the skirt is still in the air and not touching the ground. Otherwise, stumbling or falling is unavoidable.

11) Dotting

Travelling to the side with one foot on a quarter rise and the other on the flat, the dancer must control the absolute smoothness of the movement (as in gliding) while the hands perform sharp flicking movements. That effect is achieved by executing very small steps and by pulling down the shoulder blades, while holding up the chest as well as controlling the diaphragm and abdominal muscles.

12) Lilts (3/8)

The arms move smoothly – as if 'floating over the waves' – and their action is initiated by the impulse given from the top of the back and the slight bounce of the knees.

13) *Pas de Basque* and hand flicks

These steps are performed with spirited and very jagged movements. To avoid getting into trouble with the long skirt, one has to apply the same technique as mentioned in the '*développé* walks'.

14) *Renversé* turns

In this *renversé* turn, the torso and arm movements are more important than the speed. The first movement of the lifted knee must be fast and sharp (as in some of the previous movements described) in order to avoid stepping on the skirt and stumbling.

15) Revolving turns

The turn – as its name suggests – is executed by placing more body weight on the opposite leg (revolving leg) from the direction of the turn. The steps on the flat feet are kept tiny and fast and the head is not spotting. It is nice to finish the revolving action with a Georgian bow (as practised at the barre).

16a) Fruit picking (oranges from trees)

This is a mime exercise though strongly stylised. The head must be held *en face* (as if an imaginary basket is placed on the dancer's head) and only the eyes look in the direction of the working hand as if watching the action of picking. Afterwards the eye-focus drops downwards to indicate the next action, when the hand will be throwing the fruit into the basket. As in oriental mime, it is a general rule that the eye movements serve as an indicator for the next action.

16b) Fruit picking (berries from bushes)

As this time the imagined basket is placed on the hip, the head and eyes can move and be directed where the hand is working. An expression of satisfaction is emphasised by dropping the head slightly forward and then lifting it after each 'picking' of a berry from the bush.

RUSSIAN STYLE

When teaching this style, one should remember that the Russian Empire before the First World War, and during the long decades of the Soviet Union, was made up of numerous nations and ethnic minorities (such as Georgia, Ukraine, Uzbekistan, Afghanistan, Kazakhstan, and so on). These people had their own language, folklore, music and, naturally, their own dance traditions. Usually, under such historical and geographical circumstances, it is natural that some cultures influence one another. Although they might have created political turmoil from time to time, from a cultural point of view it didn't have always a negative outcome.

Consequently there are now quite a few steps in Russian dancing that were 'borrowed' a long time ago from some of the dance cultures of these ethnic groups, but by changing an accent or by adding a typical Russian arm movement, they became 'Russian-ised' and influences happened, of course in both directions. The 'running *pas de Basque*' (or *promenade*) from the Ukraine is a good example. However, as the vocabulary is vast, it is advisable to teach (for the 'non specialist' students) only the most typical movements of this style and their relevant barre exercises.

It is also a fact that some of the most artistic, professional and semi-professional dance ensembles from the Soviet Union that toured the world have shown various dances that were choreographed with a specific meaning (eg the 'Partisan' dance, 'Sailors' dance, 'Football match'). In these compositions, the choreographers used several 'borrowed' movement-elements that helped to express the subject of the choreography. One must distinguish which these movements are and, even if they are spectacular steps, they needn't be included in the class.

RUSSIAN STYLE CLASS

BARRE EXERCISES

All the barre exercises prepare the dancer not only to be able to perform Russian dancing in the correct style, but also to have the stamina to do so. However, one has to keep in mind that the dancers' muscles should be kept aesthetically pleasing and injury avoided.

For the sake of the style most of these exercises have to be executed on *demi-plié demi-pointe,* hops on *relevé demi-plié,* on f*ondu* and – for the male dancers – hops in *grand plié.*

Therefore, each of the barre exercises – though repeated several times and at different speeds – should be arranged by the teacher in such a way that, within an *enchaînement*, the weight is taken regularly off the supporting leg. Stamina and strength has to be achieved gradually and safely. It is important also that the movement of the torso, head and arm is used in a co-ordinated and natural way. Over-straining the calf and thigh muscles must be avoided, and it is especially important to check the use of correct breathing.

1) *Révérence*
2) **Preparation for all barre exercises**

This *port de bras* starts with a strongly emphasised impulse movement downward with the palm facing forward, while the head is lifted powerfully upwards. The arm continues its progress first upwards and then downwards with an evenly controlled, smooth and circular *en dedans* movement, whilst the head drops slightly downwards until the hand arrives at the height of the hip. The knuckles are placed with emphasis onto the hip and the head is lifted up simultaneously into a *petit épaulement.*

As in other classes, the notated Russian style class follows the custom of practising *battement tendu* before *pliés*. In this instance, however, we present the more traditional order of exercises here as there are a number of different *battement tendus* described.

RUSSIAN STYLE

3) *Pliés* (in 2nd position also performed in 1st, 4th and 5th)

In this style it is typical that the *demi-* and *grand pliés* are executed with an initial downwards impulse together with the arm and head movement. But immediately the leg – like the accompanying *port de bras* – proceeds with the utmost control downward while the weight of the body is kept up. The movement gives the impression of dropping, but in fact it is only doing so for a fraction of a second and from then on it is very much controlled. Placing the knuckles on the hip while lifting the head is always done with definition.

4a) *Battement tendu* A

A common fault is that the dancer, instead of bending precisely to the side over the working leg, leans into a kind of *écarté* in front of the leg. Also, it is very important that the shoulders are pulled down and the elbow is not dropping backwards.

4b) Heel *battement tendu* B with small *développé*

After the dancers have learnt the simple version of this movement, they can practise it so that when they close the position, they do it with a little stamp on the floor. Another version is that the stamping on the floor is not on the flat foot but on the heel. Later one can practise this *tendu* alternating the versions and at different speeds.

4c) *Battement tendu piqué* (not Benesh notated)

Battement tendu piqué involves the working leg touching the floor with the toe and the heel, with the accent on the 'up', and light movements. Can be interspersed with retiré.

5a) *Battement tendu jeté* A

The working leg performs this movement with a light and swinging quality whilst the footwork is sharp and crisp.

5b) *Battement tendu jeté* B

The lifting of the shoulder/shoulders might express a kind of 'cheekiness' (when the girls do it) or a kind of 'showing off' (when male dancers do it).

RUSSIAN STYLE

6) *Rond de jambe à terre*

When teaching this exercise it is best to concentrate first on the working leg and its footwork. This is one of those rare exercises when the working foot has to be slightly 'sickled' while it 'embraces' the supporting ankle and continues its movement on the floor in *croisé* on the outside edge of the foot. One has to do this 'sickled' position of the foot with moderation and control. Then teach separately the *demi-plié* with the version on the supporting leg, and only then practise the full version with both feet.

7) *Pas tortillé*

This exercise can be practised first by executing the footwork in even time and then with various rhythms. It is a good preparation for the popular 'Snake step' danced in many versions in the centre by both genders.

8) 'Snake' step (analysed)

This step is very popular and is used in the centre with sideways travel and in a circle and at various speeds and rhythms. It can be used at the barre by executing it in a small circle when turning to the other side. It can be practised so that the *demi-plié* is kept while progressing in the circle, or one can 'bounce' on the *demi-plié*. Arms can be placed in the front of the chest at shoulder level holding the elbows.

9) *Flic-flac*

When teaching this movement it is advisable to break it up into several phases. First do the supporting foot's heel lifts tapping with clear and audible precision. Then practise separately the footwork of the working leg. Then start first with the supporting leg working alone a few times indicating the speed and pulse of the movement (like a metronome) and, when this becomes natural and mechanical, add the movements of the working leg.

10) *Battement fondu*

It is important that when holding the leg in the lifted *à la seconde* position, the body weight and the balance line is comfortably over the *relevé* of the supporting leg so the hand can be lifted off the barre. While on balance, the dancer may execute claps in given rhythms.

11) *Grands développés soutenus* (men)

This is the same exercise as was practised previously as *Battement tendu* B, now done with the working leg reaching the height of over 90 degrees. Naturally the tempo is somewhat slower than in the *battement tendu* version.

12) *Grand battement*

13) *Grand changement*

This exercise should be first practised facing the barre, holding it with both hands so that the dancers learn how to control landing onto the *demi-plié relevé* without hurting themselves. This movement has a lower and faster version that can be danced by both genders.

Preparations at the barre for male dancers' *Grand Allegro*.

The next exercises must be practised for a while facing the barre and not repeated too many times in one go. In between these exercises the dancers should be given some rest. At a later stage, these movements should be executed standing sideways to the barre, and supported only by one arm. When they feel safe, they can practise them in the centre.

14) *Grand battement*

This exercise can be practised with some slaps on the inside of the boots, and also in combination with some *retirés, battement tendus* or any other movements which are not too strenuous.

15) *Plisadska* (men) A and B

The hold on the barre must be quite light. A common fault is that the dancer tries too hard, holding his breath in a panicky strain. Wrong breathing makes the muscles tighten up and this results in cramps. The dancers must hold their torso erect, breathing freely, with their shoulders locked downwards and their chest lifted. To move their legs fast and easily they must use their abdominal muscles.

CENTRE EXERCISES

16) *Promenade* **2/4**

17) *Promenade* **3/4**

When dancing by oneself, all the above-described versions of the *promenade* can be performed with various arm positions by both genders. (E.g. knuckles on the hips; arms bent and with hands touching the opposite elbow; arms stretched downwards in a low diagonal with palms turned forwards.) Male dancers (can) have their arms behind their backs with the hands flat over the sacroiliac.

All these steps can also be danced with dancers together holding hands, crossing arms behind their backs or touching each others' shoulders.

18) Slow walks (ladies)

This step can be performed in all the versions as described above in the '*promenade*'.

19) 'Running' *promenade*

In order to achieve speed, the dancer must lean backwards in *épaulement* (using the diaphragm and the back muscles). While the legs do the abrupt steps, the *port de bras* remains in the open position with head held.

20) Pivots

Sometimes this step is performed turning on the spot and also travelling sideways while keeping the movements on one level. Other times it is done emphasising the *demi-plié* action and faster travelling. Females often hold their arms bent in front of the chest, resting one elbow on the other arm's hand and with the chin of their tilted head nesting between the first and second finger.

21) Dotting (ladies)

Most of the time this step is danced by the female dancers, but it can be also performed by men. The quality of the movement is mostly lyrical and smooth. It is usually accompanied with slow and continuously flowing Russian *port de bras*.

22) Rocking A and B

The small rocking step – danced by both genders – is kept all the time in a *demi-plié* with the arms usually in the 'Russian' arm-position (elbows held in front of the chest). In the large rocking step, the arms are held in low diagonals with the palms turned forwards. Male dancers usually do it with a quite-highly lifted leg, while female dancers don't lift the leg higher then 60 degrees.

23) Tap springs

This step is danced by both genders. One can perform it on the spot or travelling to the side. It is executed with turned-out legs. A common mistake is that too much weight is put on the 'tapping' foot and so it becomes a rather heavy stamping. It must be performed with sharp, but light, movements at an absolute steady speed. The quality of this step is – to use an expression from the world of music – 'staccato' and not 'tenuto'. The arms can accompany these steps with the 'preparation *port de bras*' learnt with the barre work or held in the 'Russian' arm position.

24) 'Hop heel' step *enchaînement* (heel beating)

At the beginning, it is advisable to break down the *enchaînement* which is mostly performed as a choreographic phrase travelling forwards. Although the basic 'hop-heel' step looks quite different from the above described 'tap-springs', its technical principle is based on the same idea. The dancer must not put weight onto the tapping foot, but keep it over the hopping one, and the quality of the steps and hops is 'staccato' and not 'tenuto'. To accompany this *enchaînement,* one can use the shoulder lift that was learnt at the barre in the *battement tendu jeté* exercise.

25) Heel *Pas de Basque*

This movement is performed with lightness but at the same time with controlled force.

26a) Virvyiovoshka (The literal translation is 'A piece of string')

This is perhaps one of the most known and popular steps in Russian dancing. Looking at it superficially it is similar to its Hungarian Court style relative, though it has to be performed with an entirely different technique and style. This skipping step is danced all the time with deep *demi-plié and* on *relevé,* while its Hungarian counterpart is executed with straight knees. The torso is kept mostly *en face* (contrary to the Hungarian Court style) while the arms can be held in the same typically Russian positions that were described previously.

26b) Double Virvyiovoshka

In order to avoid heavy and sticky execution of this fast and 'staccato' step, the dancers' technique – as in the various tapping steps studied before – is based on the same principal idea. The weight of the body has to be over the leg that is in front, hopping, maintaining the *demi-plié relevé* so that the double taps of the leg behind can be light and crisp. The top is held erect with shoulders locked downwards.

27) 'Snake step'

This movement is very popular in both lyrical and vivacious dancing. It has slow and fast versions. It can be performed with changing rhythms, with a smooth or a bouncy quality, turning, circling or sideways moving and with the various *port de bras* that are typical in the Russian style. It is danced by both genders.

28) *Grand Pas de Basque* (men)

The legs are lifted quite high in this jump. There are several versions of how to execute touching the floor with the foot descending from height onto the heel (with or without making a sound); with the foot flat (with or without making a sound) or onto the toe. It is important to practise all versions, but perhaps the most useful is to learn how to execute it without making the sound. This interpretation teaches the dancer how to control an energetically descending leg from 'dropping' down heavily. With this technique, they also learn how not to damage the sensitive foot and toe joints. Male dancers should execute these with high jumps and highly lifted legs. (In this case the speed must be slower.)

29) *Temps de flèche (men)*

When executing the *attitude croisée derrière* while sliding and stamping backwards, the arms must forcefully swing next to the body *en dedans* down and again upwards behind a forward and upwards lifted torso. Though mostly danced by men, sometimes ladies perform it also but with a somewhat lower *attitude* position.

30) Plisadzka (men)

Dancing in full *plié,* which the dancers have already practised at the barre, should also be practised in the centre, as this technique is necessary for male dancers not only in the Russian character dances but also in numerous of the classical ballet traditions (Petrushka*,* Firebird, etc.) However, it has to be very gradually introduced into the centre work and the *enchaînements* must be created in such a way that other steps, that are not executed in *grand plié* position, are mixed with the movements that are done in full *plié*. It is advisable to practise these towards the end of the class, when the dancers' bodies are most pliable but not yet exhausted.

31) *Temps levé sauté* A and B (men)

In both versions, one must concentrate not only on jumping high, but also strive to stay in the air for a second at the height of the jump, by keeping the breath held whilst lifting the chest with the shoulders pulled down.

Pirouettes

32a) *Pirouette en dedans*

Perhaps the *en dedans* turns are more typical of this style, but the male dancers especially do *pirouttes en dehors* as well. Whichever is the case, there is a general rule:

the *demi-plié* and the arm position of the preparation should be executed very fast and it must not be 'obvious'. A common mistake, amongst the men, is that they hold their hands in a tight fist. The fingers have to be in a rounded position, but definitely not clenched.

32b) *Pirouettes en dehors*

Diagonal Turns

It is quite right, in this style, to use fast *chaînés* and *chassé en tournant* in the diagonal for both genders but without the use of the classical *port de bras*. Female dancers usually keep the arms straight in a low diagonal with the palms turned forwards (that helps keep their skirts from lifting too much) or the knuckles on their hips. The male dancers might have both arms in 2nd position. These arm positions are used in all types of diagonal turns (running and skipping).

33) Virvyiovoshka turns

One can alternate slow turns with double fast ones, and vary the arm positions as well. Keep the 6th position all the time, and the knee must not be lifted too high.

34) *Chassé coupé en tournant*

Ladies usually do this version with one arm lifted in 5th position or with knuckles on the hip, while gentlemen put both arms in 2nd position.

All these turns can be finished off with some *chaînés* and/or multiple *pirouettes*.

ROMANIAN STYLE

Due to its history and geography, one finds many different cultural traditions in Romania. After the end of the First World War, the country became much larger with a more mixed population than it had before. From the Carpathian Mountains (the so-called 'Hungarian Alps') the large area called Transylvania, that already had a mixed population of Hungarians, Gypsies, and a few Romanians, was annexed to the original Romanian territory. The mixed population, which had lived there for several centuries, had themselves quite a lot of differing cultural influences.

During the Middle Ages, this part of Hungary was under the rule of the Ottoman Empire for 150 years. After this period, Transylvania again belonged to Hungarian rulers who were at the same time kings of Poland, and vice versa. So, the cultural life of Transylvania became a mixture of Hungarian, Turkish, Polish, Gypsy and Romanian traditions. Though some influence was unavoidable, each community still kept a great many of its original national culture. So, there was still a living and 'unpolluted' Romanian style in dancing and music. One of the most representative features of this style is the famous Hora.

The Hora and its music might differ somewhat from one district to another but, in principle, these dances are performed in long chains of dancers, in free (non-set) and snaking patterns. It can be danced indoors but it is even more suitable for outdoor performance. In this case, it is possible to include in it as many dancers as possible, and the more people in the Hora the more interesting the chain-patterns can be.

The music has challenging time signatures, rhythms and cross-rhythms. The soft, cat-like springy character of the steps is due to the soft footwear made out of sheepskin (similar to shoes for Scottish dancing, but rougher and more rustic), and to the rhythmically bouncing arm movements that are uniquely linked together by the little finger of each dancer's hands.

When in Western countries students study the Romanian Horas, they learn and enjoy the special qualities, unusual rhythms and musical phrasing of the style, which are completely different from ones they have seen and studied so far. Dancing the Hora, by its very nature, will teach them a lot of special skills, which are useful and important for their future in the profession. They will learn:

- to relate to each other.
- to keep the correct distances from each other.
- to concentrate on the *enchaînement* they are doing whilst watching out for the next one being shown simultaneously by the 'Hora Leader' or the 'Hora Tail'. (The Dalcroze studies spring to mind.)
- to look out for the signal to change the direction of travel.

All these studies are a good preparation for all kinds of *corps de ballet* work. Alternatively all students must be given the chance to become the 'Leader' or the 'Tail' of the Hora, so they will have the challenge of:

- improving and making up movement phrases out of the Hora's vocabulary.
- being responsible for keeping the chain unbroken while changing the patterns and directions of the Hora.

These practices are useful for the young professional and will be fun for the more mature students as well as for amateurs.

*

Right from the beginning of these studies, the female dancers should wear a few bangles on each arm, as, from the first bow through the whole barre and centre work, the dancers' arm movements correspond with the rhythmical sound they create with these bangles (Gypsy and Turkish influence).

This style of dancing is ideal to teach to junior students, but the senior generation also enjoys doing it. At the same time, it is a very suitable material to teach on Summer and Easter courses when dealing with a great number of students of all ages and standards. For the same reason it can be useful for 'end of year' school shows, open classes, etc.

ROMANIAN STYLE CLASS

BARRE EXERCISES

A bow is performed at the beginning and end of all the barre exercises.

1a) Bow A

This version of the bow is less sophisticated so it is convenient to use it during the first classes. Its correct rhythm and dynamics for both genders is used all the time in their dances. The first arm movement downwards starts with a strong impulse, from which the movement continues upwards gradually 'dying' away and slowing down. It stops for a second in the 5th position (by keeping the breath back), and then the elbow drops down heavily to the hip.

1b) Bow B

This version of the preparation is even more dynamic and technically more demanding.

2) Demi-plié

One has to pay attention to the dancers' execution of the unusual *demi-pliés* when they circle the knees in the 6th position. These *demi-pliés* are deeper than the simple ones before, and the hips must be kept facing *en face* and motionless in spite of the circling knees.

3) Full *plié*

This bending of the knees in the full *plié* is much deeper than classical ballet would allow in any position; it is more a kind of crouching movement with the top bending forwards over the fully bent legs. When the students have learnt both *demi-pliés* and the full *pliés*, they can be put together in one *enchaînement*. As the *pliés* are only performed in the 6th position, it might be enough to repeat the *enchaînement* only twice on one side and then turn immediately to repeat the whole on the other side.

4) Battement tendu

The meaning of '*tendu*' is 'stretching' (in classical ballet, the stretching of the muscles and tendons of the leg and foot). Although in the following exercises the action looks entirely different from their equivalent classical relatives (similarly to the barre exercises in the Georgian style), the actual muscle work covers completely the original meaning of the expression. The deep *demi-plié* on the supporting leg must stretch the supporting leg's Achilles tendon in a smooth way, while the other leg slides into *tendu* on the heel stretching all the muscles and tendons of the working leg and foot. (The positions of the foot suggest the Turkish influence.)

5) Lilting Step

During this movement the weight of the body must stay always on the inside leg. It is a common fault that dancers put weight on the outside foot as well at the time when there is a slight bending of both knees. (In that case the movement loses its Romanian style and becomes more like the csárdás step of the Hungarian peasant style.)

6) Demi-rond de jambe à terre

Like in the *battement tendu* the legs and feet must not be turned out. A common mistake is that the dancer slightly turns out the supporting or the working leg (or both).

7) Rond de jambe à terre

8) Petit battement

This specific exercise can be practised with or without the slight supporting knee bounces. One should perform it in different timings, rhythms and with or without the arm-shakes. Putting these variant versions in an *enchaînement* could produce quite virtuoso movements. This exercise is one of the rare ones when the slight 'sickling' of the working foot is correct. A common fault is that, in order to achieve the 'sickling' foot position, the dancer allows the whole working leg to turn out. The lifted thigh in front must be kept in a parallel position while only the lower leg is slightly turned out. These movements can be used later in the Hora.

In its static form they are used mostly without beating the supporting leg, rather as skips with *petits ballonés*.

9a) *Rond de jambe en l'air* A with *rond de pied*

9b) *Rond de jambe en l'air* B with *plié*

This exercise is – like the previously described *petit battement* – performed with or without supporting knee bounces: with or without *rond de pied*. This is one of the rare cases in this style where the working leg and its flexed foot is turned out each time when finishing the *rond*. Later one can combine these movements with some *petits battements*.

10) *Grand battement balancé*

The co-ordination of the arm, torso, head, supporting knee-bounces and the swinging movements of the working leg is most important. The foot is held in the so-called 'oriental position'; arching the instep, but at the same time curling the toes upwards.

11) Break

This step is often used in the centre before changing directions, or as a rest after a long time dancing. It can be performed with the arm movement of the preparation as well.

CENTRE PRACTICE

All steps described in the following notation are performed by both genders. It is advisable to ask the dancers practising the Hora not to wear rings, as experience shows that moving the arms while being linked with the other dancers by the little fingers can cause pain and bruising.

12a) Walking step A (link little fingers)

The dancers must learn to roll on their feet when walking forwards and backwards while keeping their upper legs fairly close together.

- When walking forwards, roll from the heel to the ball of the foot. The torso leans backwards.
- When walking backwards, roll from the ball of the foot onto the heel. The torso is slightly bent forwards.

12b) Walking step B (link little fingers)

When the technique of the soft rolling footwork is achieved, the dancers should combine walking forwards and backwards with bouncing from the knee on each step, and the use of bouncing arm movements as well as the correct use of the top and head. Later the walks can be practised at different speeds; in different rhythms; running instead of walking; changing the direction of the steps or runs, and finally changing the direction of the Hora.

13a) *Chassé-coupé-chassé*

This step can be danced with or without linking fingers and by both genders. When not linked together with the other dancers, the individual often places both arms behind the torso onto the sacroiliac. Female dancers often do this movement with the special 'oriental' *port de bras* as if moving a veil in front of their faces (a remnant of Turkish influence). This step can be performed with linked hands, changing speed, time signatures ... the variations are endless but whatever the version the *épaulement* must be very much emphasised.

13b) With *port de bras*

14) *Ballonnés*

This step is based on the *petit battement* exercise at the barre, but performed without beating the supporting leg with the working foot, and executed with a small *jeté* onto the supporting leg. It is usually done while travelling to the side, and is combined with some walking steps also travelling to the side while facing towards the centre of the circle. One can do various arrangements, according to the timing and the number of linking steps, as well as how many *petits-ballonés* are performed between the linking steps. The character of this *enchaînement* is fast and crisp.

ROMANIAN STYLE

15a) Big skips

15b) Big skips with runs

The preparation for this step at the barre was the *grand battement balancé,* but in the centre, – instead of the knee bounces on the supporting legs, one performs high skips. The height of these skips is helped by the *port de bras.* As a rule, after performing two 'big skips' (*croisé* and *effacé*) there are a few 'walking steps' with knee bounces performed before repeating the phrase. The number of linking steps and their direction depends on the decision of the Hora leader (choreographer or teacher).

16) Loops

Various timings and patterns

This is also a variation on the 'Walking step' (forward/backwards and slow/fast) while facing the centre of the circle and making progress to the side. The variations are endless. The more dancers perform this version and the larger the studio (stage) is, the more variations in floor pattern (speed, direction of steps, direction faced, rhythms) can be performed, either with linking hands or individually.

HUNGARIAN PEASANT STYLE

In general this style – similarly to the Romanian – is very far from classical ballet. However, bearing in mind that it is taught to the youngest classically trained pupils of a professional school, the character class in the Hungarian Peasant style has to be built on a base that is physically safe and understandable for the youngsters. It needs to be danced with a simple and 'down to earth' quality. When performing it, the idea must be that 'the less sophistication, the better'. It doesn't demand great technical challenge or physical strength, and therefore is suitable for the youngest age group.

The traditional dances vary in style from district to district, as is the case in every country. They also depend on the occasion at which they are performed (e.g. weddings, celebrating May, various harvests and christenings). Then there are the various occupational dances of cowboys, herdsmen, recruiting soldiers, and cooks. The style of the dances also depends on the objects they dance with (bottle, candle, spoons, branches and so on), and the movements are influenced by the traditional costumes of each specific district; boots, shoes, spurs, slippers, short or long skirts and the type of headdress).

Sometimes they dance in pairs, other times in a circle, in straight lines and a horseshoe pattern, either of one gender or both. The men dance with great vigour, with lots of slaps and taps on their boots, finger-clicks and heel-clicks. However, high jumps or pirouettes of any kind are not typical.

The women might dance holding a handkerchief in their hand; with a bottle on their head or with wooden spoons. Their dancing can be vivacious but is more modest then the style of the men. Often the quality of the ladies' dancing is lyrical and tender – but never sentimental!

HUNGARIAN PEASANT STYLE CLASS

BARRE EXERCISES

1) Preparation for all barre exercises

(Handkerchief for girls)

The girls do this 'waving' arm movement with or without a handkerchief held between their first and second fingers. If held, they flick the hand from the wrist sharper in order to move the hanky with it. After the 'waving', the hand is placed on the hip with the thumb behind while the palm and the four fingers are resting in front of the hip (with or without the hanky). It is important that, when holding the arm in this position, the elbow doesn't drop backwards and the shoulders are pulled down. The boys can do the *port de bras* with a finger click or without, and place the hand either on the hip (like the girls), or behind their torso with the hands resting flat against the sacroiliac.

2) *Battement tendu* A

The *demi-plié* in the 6th position, while leaning forward with the top and turning the head sideways, is a very basic position in this style. It is called Kukkó in the Hungarian language and it means a kind of crouching movement. The head must not be tilted either forward or backwards, the back is leaning but not bending and the elbow is never dropped back.

3) *Plié* (also performed in 1st and 5th)

The exercise is done a little faster than its classical ballet counterpart but with the same careful control of the leg muscles.

4) *Battement tendu* B (preparation for double csárdás)

The so called *demi-pliés* are rather just little bounces of the knees and they emphasise the syncopated rhythm. This technique and timing is most important when later in the centre performing the double csárdás.

HUNGARIAN PEASANT STYLE

5a) *Battement tendu jeté* A

The head and the slight upper body movements are important. (In the Russian style the top mostly leans away from the working leg; in the Hungarian peasant style, as a rule, the opposite happens.)

5b) *Battement tendu jeté* B

When the students have mastered this movement, it may be further improved by keeping the same rhythm, but, instead of doing two rises, rising only once, followed by a bouncing on the rise. Later reverse the order of the movements: start with the bounce on the rise followed by the *tendu jeté* movement. This technique and rhythm are the basis of the 'Tükör csárdás' in the centre and all its variations.

6) *Rond de jambe à terre*

All the rules which were taken into consideration when performing the *battement tendu* correctly in this style are valid in this exercise. Later one can practise it so that, after the *rond de jambe à terre en dedans,* the working leg closes with a stamp into the kukkó position. Naturally one can combine and alternate these two versions.

7) *Rond de jambe en l'air*

The dancer must keep both thighs tightly together. This way the moving leg's hamstring, as well as the 'gluteus maximus', is contracted. The more advanced version of this movement is that while the *rond* is performed, the supporting foot rises. Another variation of this exercise is that, after the rise, one 'turns in' the supporting leg just at the time when the other leg is also in a 'turned in' position.

8) *Battement frappé*

There are single and the *double frappé* exercises. It is advisable only to teach the movement forwards and backwards at first; then add the side *en dehors* followed by *en dedans* and only then *en croix*. When the students feel comfortable with this version, they may learn the *double frappé en croix*, too. Male students can do a version in which, whenever the 'turned-in' working leg is beating the supporting one, they slap the outside of the moving lower leg (boot) with the torso bending slightly forwards.

9a) *Grand battement* (boys)

Once the *grand battement* is executed forward and in the diagonal, it has to be held *en l'air* while the dancer is slapping the inside of the lower leg (boot) in the front. In the *á la seconde*, the slapping is first on the inside, then on the outside and then again on the inside. Each time after the slapping movement the arm swings freely up to the 5th position.

9b) *Grand battement* (girls)

The girls' version differs from the boys by not doing the slaps. Also, the height of the leg must be moderate.

CENTRE PRACTICE

The following steps can be danced in pairs facing each other and holding onto the waist, or with the boys holding the girls at the waist while the girls are touching the boys on their shoulders. They can do the steps to the same side or the opposite. All versions of the csárdás step can be also be performed in a mixed gender circle dancing or performed by boys or girls alone.

10) Csárdás

This basic step can be practised in each direction, though its most popular form is travelling to the side. The steps are small. The girls can dance it flicking a hankerchief; boys can do it with a finger click or clapping.

11) Double csárdás

The accent of the movement is always on the stretching of the knees (just the opposite to the similar movements in the Romanian style). It is a common mistake to take too large steps. Also, at the time of the knee-bounce on the supporting leg, the other leg must hardly be lifted. For the boys there is a version where, each time the leg is closing in 6th position, a heel click is performed. This is particularly done in the recruiting dances (Verbunkos) when the boys are wearing spurs on their boots.

12) Tükör (Mirror) csárdás

In the centre the bounces on *relevé* are in the 6th position. In the following *demi-plié*, the supporting leg is slightly turned out while the upper leg of the lifted one is kept in the 6th, but the lower leg is slightly turned out and placed in the air across the supporting leg. A frequent mistake is to put the working leg in a small *attitude devant*. When the step is reversed, the upper leg is next to the supporting one in 6th position, while the lower leg is across at the back (similar to the position in the *rond de jambe en l'air* barre exercise.) These details have to be practised with precision, in order to have no difficulties in performing the Tükör (mirror) csárdás diagonal turns.

13) Cifra

This step is danced in all the Hungarian folklore dances and by both genders in all kinds of variations. It is performed facing *en face, effacé, écarté, croisé;* on the spot; travelling forwards or backwards; in couple dancing; in circle dances. It can also be executed so that (on the second beat) either the heel or the ball of the foot or the toes are placed on the floor. In the *effacé* version *after* the little jump, usually the landing onto the *fondu* is soft and deep. The emphasis of the whole step is down to earth, while the other versions are performed with an upward tendency.

14) Twisting step Hegyező

A common error is that the dancer puts weight on the ball of the front foot. The whole weight of the body must be over the back leg that should be on a full *relevé*. The arms are held in 5th position and, although they appear to move, they are motionless and only the hands are making slight waving movements. It is the twisting action of the torso that makes it seem that the arms are involved. It is danced by both genders.

HUNGARIAN PEASANT STYLE

15) Rida

This basic step is also performed in many different versions by boys and girls, but perhaps favoured more by the latter. It occurs mostly in circle dances facing towards the centre of the circle; travelling fast or slow while bending slightly forwards or backwards; simply holding hands; holding hands across the waist in front or behind holding onto shoulders. The girls often perform it in a lyrical mood, but it might also be danced also quite vivaciously.

16) Rida turns

Mainly performed by girls when coupled with boys. The boys' right arms are in 5th position while holding and lifting the girls' hands and letting them turn under their arms. The turn can be executed also as a diagonal turn. In this case, the girl performs it by herself with arms either both hands on the hip or with one arm up in 5th position while flicking the handkerchief. The turn can be either *en dedans* or *en dehors*. The latter version is the more popular.

17) Cifra turns

With each Cifra, one does only a half turn with the first one *en dedans* and so forth. The dancers (both genders) may do the turns with either the heel or the ball of the foot on the floor.

18) Tükör (mirror) csárdás turns

These turns can be danced by both genders. Half a turn is performed on each Tükör csárdás, the first one being *en dedans*. At a more advanced level, one may do an *enchaînement* in such a way that, after two half turns, one does a *relevé* with a bounce in the 6th position followed by a *tour en l'air*. Girls do a single one while boys do a *double tour*. The *tour en l'air* lands in a 6th position *demi-plié*. Then repeat the whole *enchaînement* several times.

www.ingramcontent.com/pod-product-compliance
Lightning Source LLC
LaVergne TN
LVHW051056080426
835508LV00019B/1907